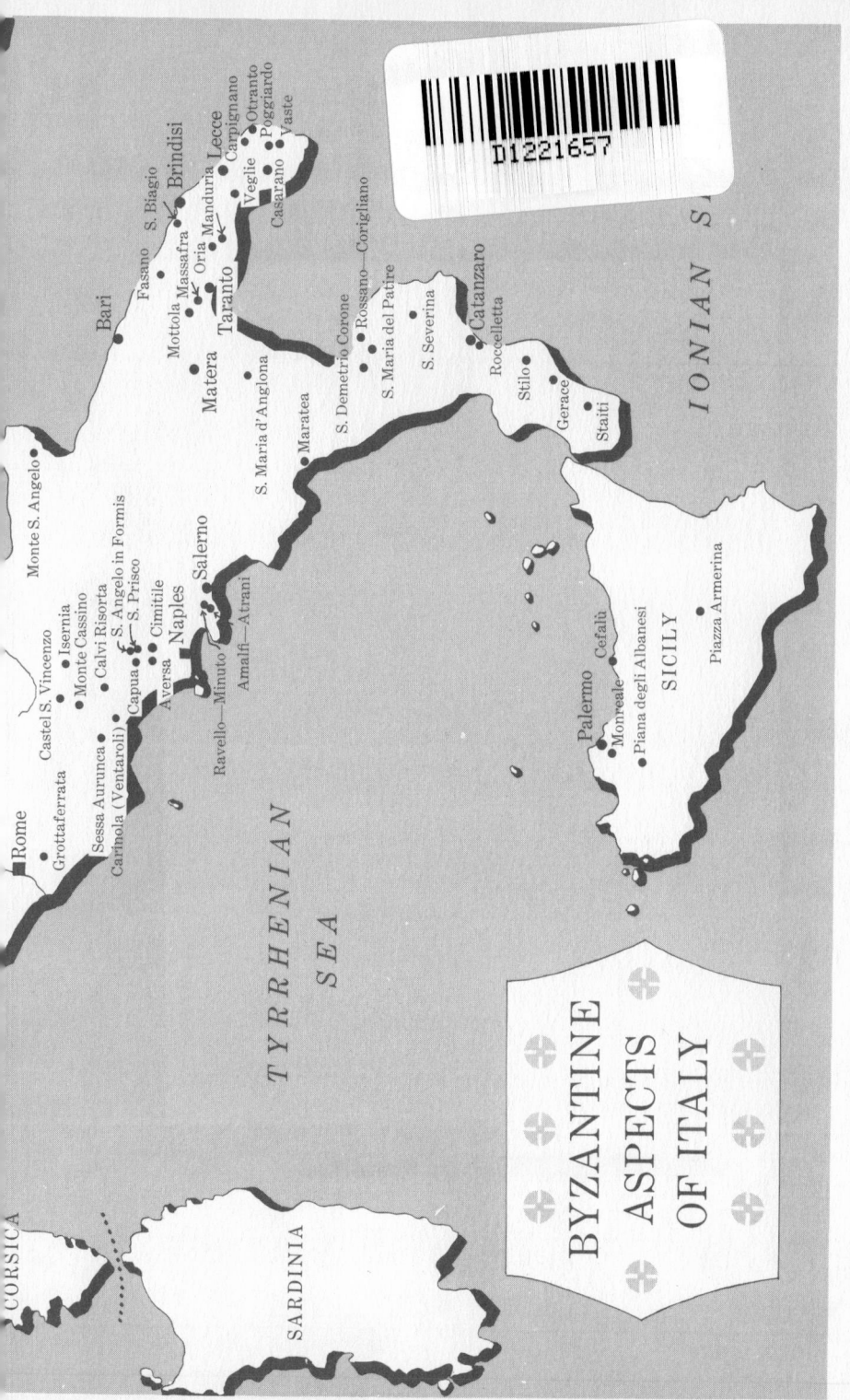

BYZANTINE ASPECTS OF ITALY

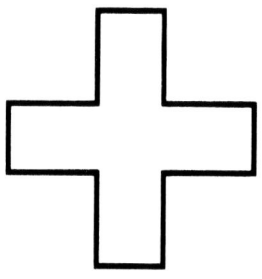

BYZANTINE ASPECTS OF ITALY

BY *Daniel Crena de Iongh*

BYZANTINE
ASPECTS
OF ITALY

New York W·W· NORTON & COMPANY · INC ·

FIRST EDITION

Copyright © 1967 by W. W. Norton & Company, Inc. All rights reserved. Published simultaneously in Canada by George J. McLeod Limited, Toronto. *Library of Congress Catalog Card No. 67-19211.* Printed in the United States of America.

1 2 3 4 5 6 7 8 9 0

To MY WIFE, my companion on our Byzantine travels
and on the great voyage of life

CONTENTS

PREFACE

Long before Constantine settled on the Bosporus at the entrance of the Golden Horn, a Greek colony called Byzantion had been founded there. This colony passed through many vicissitudes before becoming, in the first century after the birth of Christ, part of the Roman Empire. In the course of its history it had profited—though also suffered—from its enviable location; but its stature as Constantine's residence was the source of its eventual greatness. From being an outpost of the Roman Empire it became a center, and, after six years (324–30) during which Constantine's building activities turned Byzantium into Constantinople, the city proved to have become not one of those synthetic capitals we sometimes see emerging today, but a real capital in the broad sense of the word. The combination of its incomparable geographic location and its new dignity as the seat of an emperor provided an excellent base for the political, military, economic, and cultural activities that the highly centralized Eastern-oriented Roman Empire was to pursue.

It was to become the inspiring center of the empire's strength, culture, and spirituality. The component parts of the empire, so unlike each other, were tied together by this center, which both inspired them and fascinated Byzantium's enemies.

It is natural to start studying such an empire from its center. But in order to understand the impact of the capital on the out-lying areas in various periods, it is important to study the periphery and its varying relations with the capital. The cultural influence of Byzantium was by no means limited by the empire's factual or legal power, so that anyone studying Byzantine monuments in the periphery or even beyond the empire's border is bound to encounter a complicated situation.

Of this, Italy provides a special example. It was the main territory of the western portion of the empire and the land where Rome lay—the glorious world capital, residence of the popes. Despite the transfer to the east of the principal administrative body and the domicile of the emperor, and even after the barbarians again occupied it in greater part after Justinian's reconquest, Italy continued to be an important factor for the Christian empire Byzantium was. Furthermore, parts of Italy remained in Byzantium's hands until around the turn of the millennium. Even after their loss, Byzantium and Italy, for better or for worse, kept influencing each other.

In dealing with those monuments in Italy that demonstrate Byzantine influences, one must realize that Rome, Milan, Ravenna, Venice, the South, and Sicily, where such monuments are preserved, are not only different and separate subjects in themselves, but each of these again shows different aspects reflecting different periods in their histories.

In the course of many travels in "Byzantium," several trips have taken us into "Byzantine" Italy. Locating each monument and correctly pinpointing its connection with Byzantine influence is, in fact, a highly intricate matter. A great many specialized and schol-arly books have been written on specific Byzantine and Byzantine-oriented monuments in Italy; excellent guidebooks also, though these latter, in describing such monuments, mix them in among the vast number of generally interesting things to be seen in that country. The traveler in Italian Byzantium needs all these sources to arrive at a satisfactory Byzantine-oriented program. Such work is difficult and time-consuming, but it is rewarding. It goes without saying that some general grasp of Byzantium's political history and religious background is basic to the undertaking.

It occurred to us that the result of our own preparations, combined with some account of actual visits to the monuments herein described, might be helpful to other travelers in this realm. May this small volume, destined by an amateur of Byzantium for others of like kind, lead them to enjoy visits to the churches and hermits' caves, as well as the museums, where Byzantine mosaics, frescoes, sculptured objects are to be found. For those who wish to follow the subject further with the reading of specialized books, many of the best and most easily accessible are discussed at the end of the volume.

The Byzantine traveler will gradually become familiar with the Eastern way of presenting particular biblical scenes and personalities in fresco and mosaic. He will soon recognize the balding St. Paul with his dark beard and little topknot, whether ceremoniously introducing a saint to Christ or just in the process of being lowered from the walls of Damascus in a basket; St. Peter with his curly gray locks, the good St. Nicholas with his small mouth, the young St. Demetrius in his garb of the warrior-saint, St. Panteleimon with his pointed chin, and many others with whom he will find himself more closely involved than he would ever have thought possible.

Take your Bible along on the trip! It will add greatly to your enjoyment and understanding to look up the texts indicated in the following pages, for since most of the mosaics, frescoes, and sculptures are concerned with religious subjects, the Bible will bring to life the background of all you see.

ACKNOWLEDGMENTS

THE KIND GUIDANCE of various Byzantine scholars was of great value to me when at a ripe age I found myself interested in Byzantium. I am deeply obliged to them.

In the preparation of this book I feel greatly indebted to Ivanka Nikolajević of the Byzantine Institute of Belgrade, Yugoslavia, for her kindness in reading the manuscript and making constructive suggestions, as well as to my wife, M. D. Herter Norton, from whose wide editorial experience the book has so much profited.

Special appreciation is due to the efficient assistance of the staff of W. W. Norton & Company, Inc., in preparing the manuscript for the press and in particular to the interested and competent craftsmanship of David P. Hamilton.

BYZANTINE ASPECTS OF ITALY

The Emperor Justinian (mosaic in San Vitale, Ravenna)

I

INTRODUCING
BYZANTIUM

IN THAT FAMOUS WORK, *The Decline and Fall of the Roman Empire,* written between 1776 and 1788, Gibbon dealt with the history of Byzantium as merely part and parcel of Rome's decay. For nearly a century this sweeping assumption, although not in accord with the views of many earlier authors, seems to have received general acceptance. Then, toward the last quarter of the 19th century, thinking turned to question Gibbon's stand. Had not Byzantium, though an offshoot of Rome, ever taken on a character of its own? Was nearly a thousand years not a rather long time for a continuing decline and fall, a process that besides had already been going on in Rome itself for quite a time? Did not what was happening yonder on the Bosporus indicate the development of a new entity with a soul of its own, inherently different from the Western Empire?

For many, the answer to these questions was positive. The new entity had its own periods of glory as well as of decline, and, alas, also its fall. A new discipline arose: the study of Byzantium—of a fascinating period of history, religion, and art, which in the course of astonishingly few years has opened up a large field of interest and high specialization.

The transfer of the center of government of the Roman Empire to the Bosporus by Constantine the Great (324–37) signalled the beginning of a fundamental change in its history. From then on, several forces started to mold a new entity. The three factors that gave Byzantium its character were, as Ostrogorsky points out:

1. Roman political concepts;
2. Greek culture;
3. Christian faith.

The process of development of these three elements and their molding into the new entity was of course gradual, and the Byzantines, who simply continued to call themselves Romans, were not aware of the birth of a new nation on any specific date. Historians generally consider the interaction of these elements as having led to something distinctively new by the time of the death of Justinian the Great, sometimes called the last Roman emperor, in 565. While some advocate an earlier date, others a later, anyone concerned with things Byzantine is interested in following up the process of the merging of the three elements, whether this was completed before Justinian's death or after. The development of Christianity and Christian art are of special interest to the Byzantine-oriented student.

Though Christianity was born in the East, Italy played a prominent role early in its development, particularly as Rome was the city of the popes. It was the Christian art of Rome that provided the basis on which Byzantine art began, and this latter, centered to a great extent in Constantinople, came in its turn to influence Italy. This influence was felt not only in those parts of Italy still or once again dominated by Byzantium, but also indirectly in the parts where Byzantium had no power at all—Normannic Sicily, for instance, which at times was even at war with Byzantium. The Byzantine aspects of Italy are so intriguing because in his contacts with Byzantine-related monuments the explorer watches aspects of the various periods of Byzantine art and touches in each case, depending on time and place, upon the nature of a particular relation to Byzantium.

The creation of Byzantine or Byzantine-oriented works of art in Italy—to say nothing of the presence of imported works actually executed in Byzantium—came about under such different conditions in different periods and different parts of the country that, without some familiarity with the background formed by the main events governing the political as well as the ecclesiastical history of Byzantium and hence pertinent to the various stages of Byzantine influence in Italy, it is difficult to grasp the character of the various mosaics, frescoes, etc., that we encounter. Since Byzantine influence in Italy also differs according to geographical location, the typical features of each area, as they were affected by church and secular happenings, will be discussed in the various chapters that follow. To begin with, it may be useful to list some of the most significant of these events, as this will allow the reader to place the monuments to be seen in their correct temporal environment.

• 1 *The So-called Edict of Milan.* In 313 A.D. the emperors Constantine and Licinius met in Milan and may possibly have decided there on a policy of toleration towards the Christians. Constantine generally (but perhaps erroneously) receives the credit for this decision. In any case, it was Constantine who in 312 had introduced the Christian monogram on his standard at the battle of the Milvian Bridge in which he defeated his co-emperor and competitor Maxentius.

• 2 *The Donatist Controversy.* It was also Constantine who, in the Donatist controversy, demonstrated his belief in close ties between state and church. Since he felt that discipline in the church was necessary in the interest of the state, in his decisions between 313 and 316 he sided with the church against certain schismatic African bishops who had opposed the legality of the acts of a colleague they considered a traitor. So when in 324 he became sole emperor, domiciled in his new capital to which he gave his name, Constantine brought with him a tradition of favoring the Christian church and believing in the value of strong ties between church and state.

• 3 *The Council of Nicaea* (325). When he became sole

emperor in 324, Constantine—whether from political or from religious motives is a much-debated question—had already realized the value of Christianity as a binding force in his empire. He had shown he understood the impact any ecclesiastical dissent would have on the unity of the empire, and the consequent importance of a clear formulation of Orthodox doctrine. At the same time he laid the foundation of the imperial claim to being head not only of the state but also of the church, a thesis that was to cause many quarrels both with the patriarchs of Constantinople and with the popes, who considered themselves heads of the church, East and West.

While the Donatist controversy was important enough as a matter of church discipline, the dispute that led to the Council of Nicaea was a matter of dogma, and of the highest importance because it dealt with the very nature of Christ. It is clear that, of all Christian dogmas, the definition of the nature of Christ is of paramount significance, and dissension on this point could not be tolerated lest the church fall apart. Arius, a priest ordained in Alexandria, proclaimed that Christ, though the Son of God, was created by God and therefore could not by nature be God himself. For this he was condemned by the Deacon of the Church, the later Bishop Athanasius, and the Council upheld Athanasius's standpoint. But Arianism was not entirely stamped out and from time to time reared its head. It continued, for example, among the barbarians, particularly among the Goths, who had invaded and occupied Italy and were Christianized by Arian missionaries, thus becoming schismatics and aggravating an already difficult situation. The visitor to Ravenna will be reminded of the Arian controversy on seeing the Baptistery of the Arians, probably built by Theodoric (p. 152).

• 4 *The Council of Ephesus* (431). Nearly a century later, Nestorius, Patriarch of Constantinople, again—though in a manner less absolute than that of Arius—stressed the human nature of Christ. The Council condemned Nestorianism, stressed the divine nature of Christ, and thereby also laid the basis for the cult of the Virgin, who from now on could be worshiped as the Mother of God.

• 5 *The Council of Chalcedon* (451). Twenty years later it was Monophysitism, which, denying the dual nature of Christ and holding him to be spirit only, proved a most difficult controversy for the church to deal with, especially as the Middle

East and North Africa much inclined toward this view. The Council of Chalcedon settled the matter definitely by declaring Christ to be simultaneously God and Man. Monophysitism nevertheless came to the fore again and again. During the reign of Justinian the Great (527–65), it was to create an especially difficult problem because Justinian's wife, the famous Theodora, favored it. Only after the Empire's loss of its Middle-Eastern and African areas to Arab invasion did Monophysitism cease to recur in Byzantium.

• 6 *The Period between the Reigns of Constantine and Justinian* (337–527). This period, during which the two last-named councils took place, was politically a tragic one for Italy, where the emperors gradually lost control to the barbarian invaders. Like Constantine, Theodosius the Great (379–95) resided in Constantinople as sole emperor of the Roman Empire. But after his death the Empire was divided into a western and an eastern part, his son Honorius becoming emperor of the western part (in practice, a position without any real power), his brother Arcadius emperor of the eastern part. Honorius, whose situation in Rome had become too risky on account of the constant invasions, had set up his court in Ravenna, which, protected by its marshes, offered a safer abode. Here, after his death in 423, his powerful sister Galla Placidia took over as guardian for her minor son Valentinian, who became emperor (425–55) as a child of six. Even after he came of age, Galla Placidia must have remained the real power behind the throne until her death in 450. Daughter of Emperor Theodosius who lived in Constantinople, and educated in that city, she was imbued with the spirit of budding Byzantium: the mosaics of Ravenna ordered by her show this origin.

Theodoric, the second Ostrogoth king (493–526), had also been brought up—for political reasons, as a hostage—in Constantinople. He actually ruled Italy from Ravenna, which he managed to conquer, nominally as a vassal of the Eastern emperors, Anastasius I (491–518) and Justin I (518–27). To his Byzantine background we owe not only the mosaics of the Baptistery of the Arians but also some other Byzantine mosaics of his time in Ravenna.

• 7 *The Reign of Justinian* (527–65) *and its Consequences.* The reign of Justinian as Emperor of Byzantium had a great and restorative, though brief, influence on Italy. Although the Eastern Empire too had great difficulties with invasions, especially by the Persians in the east and the Huns in the Balkans, Justinian focused his attention on regaining the west and considered it his main task to recapture Dalmatia, Istria, Italy, and the western half of the North African coast from barbarian hands. With the help of his great general and admiral Belisarius, he succeeded in reoccupying these territories, as well as Sicily and a part of Spain, but most of these conquests proved to be short-lived.

Restoration of the old empire concentrated Justinian's attention and energies so much on the West that he did not have the power to fight the invading Persians under Emperor Chosroes I (531–79). Hence he resorted to paying them tribute, and this, having to be constantly increased, of course settled nothing, so that after Justinian's death his successors still had to cope with Persian invasions in the East, added to Slavic invasions in the Balkans. The Lombard infiltrations of Italy, which started soon after his death, took control of the greater part of that country, though Ravenna retained a dominating, albeit diminishing, power over what was left of Byzantine Italy for another 200 years. The end of Byzantine domination in Northern Italy came, as we shall see, in 751.

Justinian's interest in art gave Italy the Ravenna mosaics of his time. His tendency, like that of his predecessors, to play a role in religious matters kept alive the differences with the popes, who considered themselves heads of the church. He called the Fifth Ecumenical Council (Constantinople II, in 533) in order to condemn the religious theories of three clerics suspected of Nestorianism, hoping by this act to please the Monophysite East—an attempt which, however, did not placate the East and only aggravated the religious dissensions in the empire.

• 8 *The Arab "Explosion" after 632.* Bereft of so many of Justinian's reconquests, Byzantium was soon to lose more, and to a brand new foe—the Arabs. That vigorous people, which until then had kept within its own land, suddenly emerged soon after the death of Mohammed in 632, inspired by its new religion, to stream over all the Middle East, defeat the army of the Byzantine emperor Heraclius (610–41) and attack Byzantium's old enemies, the Persians. Egypt fell to them in 642, Cyprus in 647. Bypassing Sicily (which they attacked later, occupying nearly the whole island by the end of the reign of the Emperor Michael III, 842–67), they gradually overran all Byzantium's former African territories, by now mostly occupied by the Vandals, and reached Spain in 711. Continuing northward, they were only stopped at last in 732 at Poitiers in France, just a hundred years after their start on the path of conquest. Having also become a sea power, they twice attacked Constantinople (in 674 and 678), but they never succeeded in conquering it, its famous sea walls and other defenses proving too strong. It is probable that during this period Byzantium used for the first time its famous "Greek fire," a flaming pitch thrown on the vessels of the attacking enemy.

 • 9 *The Iconoclastic Controversy* (726–843). The widespread adoration of icons in the Orthodox Church as well as in the homes of pious citizens brought with it the danger that these representations of Christian religious motives, rather than serving as reminders of their message, tended to become objects of worship themselves—idols, in short. This danger must have been in the minds of the originators of the iconoclastic movement, but the matter became even more controversial when secular politics entered into it. The power of the monasteries—their wealth, their freedom from taxation, and the freedom of the monks from service in the army—was much criticized, and their standing was obviously much enhanced by their possession of famous icons that had become objects of adoration and were even known to have worked miracles. The army, therefore, joined the iconoclasts. The Byzantine government also thought that relations with the Arabs, who were on principle opposed to images, might be eased if iconoclasm should become an official policy.

It may be that contact with the Moslems in the Middle East had made the Byzantine emperor Leo III (717–41) sensitive to these views. He came out openly against icons and even began ordering their removal, an action that provoked the pious to revolt. Pope Gregory II (715–31) strongly condemned Leo's policies, and the Byzantine clergy, led by Germanus, Patriarch of Constantinople, and the great theologian John of Damascus, also attacked the emperor. Leo, unperturbed, ordered icons destroyed and iconodules (lovers of icons) prosecuted. When Pope Gregory III (731–41) continued his predecessor's policy, Leo put the papal legate in prison. These actions naturally led to a break between emperor and pope. Constantine V (741–75) followed in his predecessor's footsteps, convening a council in 754 that ordered the destruction of all icons, also excommunication of the Orthodox leaders and even the execution of some.

Italy was affected in several ways by this period of controversy. Around 750, Constantine V decreed that the churches in Byzantine-dominated Southern Italy should come under the patriarch of Constantinople instead of remaining under the jurisdiction of the pope, a measure that strengthened the Byzantine position in Southern Italy. In Rome the Greek population was increased by those iconodules who fled Byzantium. Furthermore, the production of Christian images and Byzantine styles was stimulated in Rome during the time when such production had ceased in Byzantium. Hence the growing influence of the Byzantine style in that period and especially during its aftermath.

Although from 780 to 813, during the reigns of iconodule rulers, iconoclasm was not practiced and although the Ecumenical Council of Nicaea II (787) showed a unanimous stand by both the Eastern and the Western Church against iconoclasm, it was not until March, 843—under the regency of Theodora, widow of the emperor Theophilus I (829–42)—that iconoclasm in the East actually came to an end.

• 10 *The Lombard Conquest of Ravenna (751) and the Formation of the Papal State.* While Justinian's successors were coping with serious difficulties in the East, the Italian part of the empire was greatly troubled by new invaders, the Lombards. In an effort to stave off this danger the Byzantine emperor Maurice (Makarios, 582–602) reorganized the Exarchate of Ravenna (the exarch being a sort of viceroy) into a military government ruling over "the province of Italy." Its powers and methods are a matter of much debate, but it is clear that the component parts of "the province," most of which could be reached only via Lombard country, differed in nature and must have made any uniform treatment very difficult. Besides Ravenna and its environs, these parts were Istria, Venice, Rimini with environs, Perugia, Rome, Naples with environs, and Calabria.

Ravenna, then, continued to exercise control over the Italian possessions of an empire not only harassed by the Lombards but obliged also to deal with the changing position of the Papacy. Byzantine power was still strong enough in 653, some hundred years after Justinian's death, for the Exarch of Ravenna to go to

Rome when so ordered by the emperor and arrest Pope Martin, whom the emperor considered rebellious. The pope was transported to Constantinople, tried, condemned, and banished to Cherson, where he died miserably in 656.

If Byzantium's "presence" in "the province of Italy" still showed its strength in Rome, where the popes were striving for independence, it would surely have kept its cultural heritage alive in that city as well. The Eastern stylistic influences of that time must have provided the basis on which a later influx of Greek elements could thrive in Rome, as we see them, for example, in S. Maria Antiqua on the Forum.

Yet the days of Byzantium in Northern Italy were numbered. In 751 the Lombards took Ravenna. Although relations with the popes were further strained when Byzantium pursued its iconoclastic policy, deeply resented in Rome, the pope had nevertheless been helping the Empire against the powerful Lombard king, Luitprandt; but this action resulted in the defeated Luitprandt presenting the regained territories to the pope. Soon after, Pope Stephen II (752–57) called on the Frankish king, Pepin, to assist in liberating Ravenna. Pepin accomplished the task, but he handed the Italian province over to the pope, not to Byzantium; and together with the previously mentioned territories it became part of the new papal state. In fact, therefore, Ravenna had been definitely lost to Byzantium in 751 and now all of Northern Italy was lost, save Venice, which was to become a vassal state of the Byzantine Empire. In the South, Naples and Calabria were from now on administered, like Sicily, directly from Constantinople.

• 11 *Charlemagne Crowned Roman Emperor (800)*. A date most important in the history of Byzantium as well as in the history of Italy was Christmas of the year 800, when Charlemagne was crowned Emperor of the Holy Roman Empire. For now there were legally two Roman Empires, the Western and the Eastern. This had no effect on Byzantium's territory in Italy, nor did Byzantium recognize the loss of its claims in the West, yet only twelve years later Charlemagne and the ambassador of the Byzantine emperor Michael I (811–13) signed a treaty at Aix in which Charlemagne was saluted by the Byzantine representative with the imperial title of "Basileus," heretofore claimed by the Byzantine emperor as his sole prerogative.

The splendor of Charlemagne's court and its treasures, let us note here, showed a taste for things Byzantine.

 • 12 *The Resurgence of the Byzantine Empire under the Amorian and Macedonian Dynasties (820–67 and 867–1056).* It was especially under Michael III (842–67) and his successors Basil I (867–86) and Basil II (976–1025) that Byzantium received a new lease on life. Although during the reign of Michael III Sicily (save for Syracuse and Taormina) was conquered by the Arabs, who could now raid Southern Italy constantly, yet the greater power of the Empire elsewhere, especially in the Balkans, made possible a strengthening and consolidation of its position even in the south of Italy. Under Basil I, Bari in Puglia was brought back under Byzantine rule at the end of 876, when it became the center of Byzantine administration in Southern Italy, replacing as such Rossano in Calabria; and it was not until nearly 200 years later, in 1071, when Bari fell to the Normans, that Byzantium was definitely pushed out of Southern Italy.

 • 13 *The Definitive Breach between the Eastern and the Western Churches (1054).* While the churches of East and West were in agreement on the big theological questions decided in the seven ecumenical councils (the last of which had been that of Nicaea II on iconoclasm, in 787), the relation between East and West had always been uneasy. The position of the Byzantine emperor in the Eastern church, as initiated by Constantine the Great; the special position of the pope; competition between the two churches in proselytizing among the Slavs in the Balkans; the authority of the patriarch of Constantinople in the south of Italy replacing, as we have seen, that of the pope; the emergence of the papal state after the fall of Ravenna—all these combined with political power conflicts to cause a growing lack of understanding between the two churches. And all this formed the background against which a number of matters of doctrine and ritual finally brought about the great break of 1054.

The main question concerned what is known as the "double procession" of the Holy Ghost: whether the Holy Ghost proceeded from God the Father alone, as the East held, or from God the Father *and* the Son ("filioque"). This point was especially galling to the East since the "Frankish" Western monks insisted on chanting the "filioque" even in the Middle East. Other questions had also come up: whether, as the East maintained, a priest could be married; the use of leavened bread in the Eucharist, as in the East, as against that of unleavened bread in the West, etc. These questions had been pending for years but now led to a rupture because of the generally bad atmosphere, aggravated by the conflicting personalities of an ambitious and hotheaded patriarch, Cerularius, and a weak emperor, Constantine IX (1042–55).

The mission sent by Rome to Constantinople, in the hope that the emperor might drop his patriarch, ended by excommunicating Cerularius and his fellow believers (probably including the emperor himself). This resulted in the patriarch, with the consent of the emperor, calling a synod that in its turn excommunicated the papal legates. The controversy, a tragic division between Christians, had grave consequences for Byzantium, especially in the period of the Crusades, which was soon to follow.

• 14 *The Normans and the Occupation of Bari (1071).* It may have been the visit to Rome of a small group of Norman pilgrims from France, offering help to the pope in his troubles with the Lombards, that led to the overmastering activities of the Normans in Italy. Whatever the beginning, the Normans became conquerors and stayed. It was they who took Bari in 1071, completing the conquest of the South, ending forever Byzantine reign in that area (p. 76). They also took Sicily from the Arabs and played an active role in the Crusades.

For Byzantium, the Normannic conquest meant more than the loss of Byzantine Italy. Bohemund, the Crusader king of Normannic Syria, attacked Byzantium in 1099. In 1107 he attacked Dyrrhachion (the present Durazzo in Albania), as he and his father Guiscard had done twenty-five years before. Bohemund lost out, and the visitor to Canosa di Puglia, seeing Bohemund's grave there and admiring the bronze doors with their Eastern motives, may meditate on what might have happened if he had been victorious at Dyrrhachion and had attained his ambition to be emperor of Byzantium. Evidently the East had had a great attraction for this Nordic Crusader king, as it had for his fellow Normans in Sicily, who, though enemies of Byzantium, adorned their palaces with Byzantine mosaics and could think of no greater glory than that of being buried in a tomb of porphyry.

• 15 *The Comnenian Dynasty (1081–1185) and the*

Crusades of 1096, 1146 and 1187. The reign of the Comnenes, coming after the weak government of the last members of the Macedonian dynasty and a short period under the dynasty of the Dukas, showed once more what competent rulers could do with a Byzantium even so much reduced. At the end of the reign of Manuel I (1143–80), the empire emerged strengthened and a little bigger, and this notwithstanding the adversities of attack from all sides by the Normans, the nomad Petchenegs of southern Russia, and the Seljuk Turks.

In fact, Byzantium's doom befell not at the hands of these enemies but as a consequence of the continued and growing misunderstanding between East and West. The Crusades, of which the first set forth in 1096, were, after all, a Western undertaking inspired by Rome. While the Byzantine emperors agreed in principle with the original purpose of the Crusaders—the recapture of the Holy Land—it was with the expectation that, as soon as these zealous fighters occupied former Byzantine territory, it would be returned to the empire. In the beginning the Crusaders themselves seemed to be of this view, but they very soon developed ambitions of their own and became, more and more, a menace to the empire.

• 16 *The Fourth Crusade (1204).* On the Byzantine side, suspicion and resentment increased, and such conditions set the stage for the Fourth Crusade to turn into an attack on Constantinople that was to degenerate into a looting enterprise.

On the 13th of April the Crusaders entered the city, the protective chain across the Golden Horn having been broken. Constantinople now became the scene of pillage on an unprecedented scale. Among the foremost beneficiaries were the Venetians: many of the objects carried off are still to be seen in S. Marco. Anyone interested in Byzantine art may be grateful to the Venetians; though it had not exactly been their purpose, they preserved for posterity, through their looting, many most beautiful objects that otherwise would probably have disappeared altogether in the final breakdown of Constantinople in 1453.

Though the Byzantine government that had lived in exile in Nicaea reoccupied Constantinople in 1261, the power of Byzantium had been broken. Ironically, though Venice had played such an important part in the destruction of Byzantium, it was in Venice for the most part, and hence through Venice, that Byzantine tradition in Italy lived on. In 1220 Pope Honorius III commissioned his mosaic in the apse of S. Paolo fuori le Mura in Rome from Venetian mosaicists, who portrayed Christ blessing *alla greca*. However, direct Byzantine stylistic influence in Italy had virtually ended.

Fish symbol (mosaic in floor of former house church in Poreć)

II

CONCERNING ICONOGRAPHY

IN ORDER TO GRASP the meaning of the early Christian monuments in Italy, one must familiarize oneself with the background of their iconography. This applies equally, of course, to the Byzantine-related monuments; through study of their Byzantine-based iconography, the visitor soon will come to recognize and distinguish the characteristic elements in the frescoes and mosaics he will encounter in his Italian journey.

Early Christian iconography in Italy is related to the period of persecution of the Christian believers who, to use a modern term, went underground. This of course accounts for the cryptic character of early Christian symbols, of which the fish is perhaps the oldest; the letters of the Greek word for fish, "ichthus," standing for the first letters of the Greek phrase "Jesus Christ Son of God

Savior." This symbol we find in the catacombs. It also appears in the remains of the "house churches," or private houses where the early Christians met to worship. We encounter remains of such house churches in Rome and in Poreč (Parenzo), Yugoslavia (p. 179).

Many of the older images do not stem from the Bible but relate rather to continuation of pre-Christian ceremonies, and were used in early Christian times as symbols of eternal life and of Christian faith. Such images show, among others:

> The pagan funeral meal, a cryptic symbol of the Last Supper (see also John 6:27).
> Peacocks with grapes, the flesh of these birds being considered perdurable and hence standing for immortality, and the grapes representing the wine of the Eucharist.
> The deceased (in the catacombs) with arms outstretched, a predecessor to the Virgin in the attitude of *orans* (praying).
> The (Greek) teacher with his pupils, a symbol of Christ and his disciples.

The next category of subjects is based on Old Testament scenes, all symbolizing eternal life:

> The four rivers of Paradise (Gen. 2:10–14).
> Noah and the ark (Gen. 6:8 and 14–22).
> The hospitality of Abraham (Gen. 18), the three angels in this story sometimes being held to foreshadow the Holy Trinity.
> Abraham's sacrifice of Isaac (Gen. 22:1–13).
> The burning bush (Exod. 3:2–5).
> Moses smiting the rock (Exod. 17:6).
> Elijah fed by the ravens (I Kings 17:4).
> Elijah fed by the widow (I Kings 17:9).
> "The Lord is my shepherd" (Ps. 23:1), precursor to the Good Shepherd.
> Isaiah's prophesy that a virgin shall conceive (Isaiah 7:14).
> The three young men unharmed in the fiery furnace (Daniel 3:12–30).
> Daniel among the lions (Daniel 6:17–24).
> Jonah and the great fish (Jonah 1:17 and 2:10).

In this category occur two subjects based on the Old Testament Apocrypha. They are the history of Susanna (originally part of the Book of Daniel) and the story of the mother of the Maccabees and her seven sons, from the Second Book of the Maccabees. According to the *Oxford Dictionary of the Christian Church*, the Old Testament apocryphal books were "received by the early church as part of the

Greek version of the Old Testament, but not included in the Hebrew Bible."

The story of Susanna and the Elders deals with a "fair woman who feared the Lord" and was falsely accused of adultery by the two elders, to whom she refused to submit. She was defended successfully by Daniel. A fresco dealing with this story we find in the catacomb of Priscilla—a symbol, again, of eternal life.

The 7th chapter of II Maccabees tells of the heroic conduct of Salomona, who urged her sons not to yield to the command of King Antiochus (one of the successors to Alexander the Great) to eat swine flesh, which meant transgressing the laws of their fathers. Inspired by their mother, they refused to submit under torture, and died before her eyes, one by one—a fate in which she followed them. We find in the church of S. Maria Antiqua in Rome a fresco dealing with this moving story, which may also be considered to symbolize eternal life and the strength of faith. Moreover, in the crypt of S. Pietro in Vincoli there stands an early Christian sarcophagus said to hold relics of the seven brothers, whose faith, though not Christian, is thus honored by Christians.

Gradually New Testament scenes appear in Italy, among them a number that are especially dear to the Orthodox Church and indicate Eastern influence:

> The Good Shepherd of Isaiah's prophecy (Isa. 40:11; also John 10:11 and 14; I Peter 5:4).
> The Transfiguration (Metamorphosis; Matt. 17:1–13; Mark 9:2–13; Luke 9:28–36); in Rome one sees this in a mosaic in the church of Ss. Nereo e Achilleo.

In this category are a number of subjects from Revelation, such as:

> The seven golden candlesticks (Rev. 2:1).
> The twenty-four elders (Rev. 4:4).
> The four beasts (Rev. 4:7), later to become the symbols of the Evangelists: the beast with the face of a man for St. Matthew, the lion for St. Mark, the calf (bull?) for St. Luke, the eagle for St. John.
> The book with seven seals (Rev. 5:1–5). In Greek iconography the book may lie, as in Castelseprio, upon the empty throne prepared for the Last Judgment (Ps. 9:8 and 103:19), sometimes with the Lamb as symbol of Christ (Rev. 5:6).
> The river of the water of life (Rev. 22:1).

These New Testament scenes later come to include the miracles of Christ, among which the following occur most frequently in the Eastern Church:

The raising of the daughter of Jairus (Matt. 9:18 and 23–25; Mark 5:22–24 and 35–42; Luke 8:41–42 and 49–56).
The two blind men healed (Matt. 9:27–31).
The feeding of the five thousand (Matt. 14:15–21; Mark 6:36–47; Luke 9:12–17; John 6:5–13).
The multiplication of the loaves and fishes (Matt. 15:33–37).
The banquet of the seven disciples at the Sea of Tiberias (John 21:1–14).
A blind man healed (Mark 8:22–25).
The miraculous draught of fishes (Luke 5:1–9).
The raising of the widow's son (Luke 7:11–14).
Turning water into wine (Marriage at Cana; John 2:1–10).
The raising of Lazarus (John 11:1–44).

Some events of the end of the life of Christ appear in the Eastern Church in a special pattern that makes their origin easily recognizable:

Christ's entry into Jericho, meeting Zaccheus the tax collector (Luke 19:1–10).
The entry into Jerusalem (Palm Sunday; Matt. 21:1–11; Mark 11:1–10; Luke 19:28–38; John 12:12–14).
The Last Supper (Matt. 26:26–29; Mark 14:22–25; Luke 22:14–20).
Peter's denial, with the cock (Matt. 26:34–35 and 69–75; John 13:36–38).
The Crucifixion (Matt. 27:33–50; Mark 15:21–38; John 19:17–36).
The Ascension (Mark 16:19; Luke 24:51; Acts 1:9).
Pentecost (Acts 2:1–13).

The iconography of the Eastern Church is itself often based on versions originating in stories of the Apocryphal New Testament. These stories have an entirely different position from Old Testament Apocryphal stories. They do not belong to the Bible but should be considered as "pious writings, some good, some bad, neither history nor religion nor even literature, but being as folklore and romance precious" (Montague Rhodes James, in his preface to *The Apocryphal New Testament*, p. xiii).

When so based, the Greek iconography often follows the Apocrypha in detail, as we see also in Italy from representations of many subjects. For example:

Joachim and Anna. The Book of James or Protoevangelium mentions Anna's immaculate conception (IV:1) and the nativity of Mary (V:2). Joachim and Anna appear in the Martorana in Palermo, flanking the main apse (p. 128).

The youth of the Virgin. These representations usually repeat the stories of the youth of Christ, such as the Presentation in the Temple (Book of James VII:2), which appears in a 17th-century mosaic on the underside of the great arch in the right transept of S. Marco in Venice.

The Annunciation. The Book of James (X and XI:1) describes how the Virgin "went to her home and set down the pitcher and took the purple [wool] and sat upon her seat and drew out the thread . . ." and the angel came and spoke to her. See the 5th-century mosaic of this scene on the triumphal arch in S. Maria Maggiore in Rome (p. 53), as well as the fine 6th-century apse mosaic in the Basilica of Euphrasius in Poreč (p. 180).

The Visitation. The visit of Mary to her cousin Elizabeth, who was to be the mother of John the Baptist, is recorded in the New Testament (Luke 1:39–45) and also mentioned in the Book of James (XII:2). Greek iconography often shows an indiscreet servant listening to the conversation between the holy women (as in the Poreč mosaic, p. 180). Can this be a spy for Herod, linked with his persecutions and the flight of both women to save their children? According to the Book of James (XXII:3), Elizabeth hid her child with the help of an angel.

The trial by water of the Virgin (Num. 5:12–31), which is also related to the Apocryphal New Testament (Book of James XVI), as in Castelseprio (p. 150).

The Nativity. A special Greek feature in the iconography of the Nativity is the washing of the Child and the appearance of Salomé, a woman who did not believe in the Immaculate Conception (Book of James XIX:2 and XX); because of her unbelief her hand began to wither, but when she repented an angel appeared, announcing that if she touched the Child it would be restored. This we see in, for instance, the Nativity at Castelseprio (p. 150).

The Dormition (sometimes called Assumption) of the Virgin. Among a number of Apocryphal texts on this subject, the version one meets in Greek icons shows the Virgin on her couch, with Christ, who has come to fetch the soul of his mother, standing behind her holding her soul like a babe in swaddling clothes, and surrounded by a host of angels. It appears in an enamel on the Pala d'oro in S. Marco in Venice (p. 165) and also in the (Italian-made) mosaics in the apse of S. Maria Maggiore in Rome.

The Anastasis (Resurrection) in the Greek version of the Harrowing of Hell (Descent into Hell or Limbo), often called the Last Judgment, to which it is closely related. This episode is based on such New Testament passages as Matt. 27:52–53 and Luke 23:43. The Apocryphal texts are far more direct and concrete on the subject and present facts in detail. There are many versions; in that of the Acts of Pilate, Latin B VIII, Christ appears standing on the broken gates of Hell, keys, bars, and hinges scattered about, with one foot on the throat of Satan, raising Adam and Eve out of Limbo (IX:1), while David (VI:1), dressed like a Byzantine emperor, stands nearby; other persons standing near Christ (also mentioned in VI:1) are patriarchs, prophets, and saints, among them Jeremiah, Isaiah, John the Baptist, and many others. The language of the stories often has a charm of its own: "then our father Adam, looking earnestly upon all the multitude, marvelled if they were all begotten of him into the world" (IV:2); and "then did the holy patriarchs begin to recognize each other and each one to speak words out of their prophecies" (VI:1). In Italy one meets this Greek (Apocryphal) version in, for example, S. Clemente in Rome (p. 67) and a panel of the Pala d'Oro in S. Marco in Venice (p. 165), as well as in a Romanesque mosaic inside the arch between the west and central cupolas of that basilica, and also in the great mosaic of the Last Judgement in the Cathedral of Torcello (p. 172).

The following two subjects, though based on the biblical version of the Last Judgment, are much used in Greek iconography and one comes to recognize the special form in which they are there presented:

The Etimasia, or Preparation of the Throne, as in Ps. 9:8, 89:15, and 103:19.
The rendering-up of the dead, according to Rev. 20:13.

Other examples of characteristic Byzantine iconography we see in Italy are:

The Deesis: Christ between the Virgin and John the Baptist. This combination of holy persons is connected with the Last Judgment, representing their intercession in favor of souls to be admitted into Paradise. See the plaque in S. Marco in Venice (p. 164).
Christ blessing *alla greca:* right hand raised, thumb, ring, and little fingers touching, first and second fingers upright, as we see it in S. Paolo fuori le Mura in Rome.

The Ancient of Days. The Eastern Church seldom portrays God directly, but occasionally uses the Old Testament figure of the Ancient of Days (Dan. 7: 9–10, 13, and 22). This we see in the grotto of S. Biagio near Brindisi (p. 114) and in the remarkable Trinity in the Convento della Favana in Veglie (p. 108).

The calendar of the great feasts of the Orthodox Church. Many of the subjects we are familiar with from the narrative cycles in mosaic and fresco belong also to the liturgical cycles depicted in this calendar. The representation of the calendar is in itself specifically Eastern. While such cycles abound in the East, often providing marginal decoration in the framing of an icon, we find them also in Italy; as on the famous bronze doors of S. Paolo fuori le Mura in Rome, on the Pala d'oro in S. Marco in Venice, on the "two elegant Byzantine miniatures in wax mosaic," as the fine portable icons in the Opera del Duomo in Florence have been called. Their subjects may vary in number from 6, 7, or 8 up to 12 and even 18. They are not always the same; they may include, for example, the incredulity of Thomas, the raising of Lazarus, the Dormition of the Virgin. The bronze doors of S. Paolo have Thomas but neither Lazarus nor the Dormition; the Pala d'oro (an incomplete cycle) has a Dormition; the portable icons have Lazarus and the Dormition but no Thomas.

Further, a number of the saints, including church fathers, that we see most frequently in Italy are specifically Eastern and may be considered to indicate Italian contacts with Byzantium. The following list is by no means exhaustive.

St. Antony (d. 356), early desert hermit. He appears with St. Paul of Thebes in the atrium of S. Angelo in Formis and in the Crypt of Ss. Stefani in Vaste.

St. Basil (d. 379), one of the three Cappadocian fathers, brother of St. Gregory of Nyssa and a friend of St. Gregory of Nazianzus, both Greek saints. He laid down the rules of Eastern monasticism (later amended by St. Theodore of Studion, d. 826); it is after him that Greek Orthodox monks are called Basilian.

Sts. Cosmas and Damian (d. ca. 300), martyr physicians from Arabia (according to legend), who practiced in Cilicia and never asked money for their services, hence being known as the holy *anargiroi*, "silverless men." As Christians they were prosecuted by Diocletian (Roman emperor, 284–305) and decapitated. They are also venerated in the West, where they became the patrons of the Medici of Florence.

St. Cyril (826–69) came with his brother Methodius from Thessalonica. They were both sent to Moravia as missionaries
in 862 by the Byzantine emperor Michael III (842–67).
Cyril is credited with inventing the Glagolitic alphabet so
that the Slavs could read the Bible in their own language.
He died in Rome and was buried in the church of S.
Clemente (p. 67).

St. Demetrius (d. 303), a warrior saint venerated especially in Thessalonica, was martyred by Diocletian for his Christian faith.

St. George (d. 303) was also martyred by Diocletian. He is mostly
depicted on a white horse, killing a dragon, and is also
much venerated in the West.

St. Gregory of Nazianzus (329–89), like St. Basil one of the Cappadocian fathers, a great theologian and a great influence
in restoring the Nicene Creed, leading to its final establish-
ment at the Council of Constantinople in 381.

St. Gregory of Nyssa (330–95), brother of St. Basil, the third of the
Cappadocian fathers, a great thinker and theologian and
defender of the Nicene Creed.

St. Helena (255–330), Constantine the Great's famous and powerful
mother, venerated for her piety, in her old age visited the
Holy Land, founded the basilica on the Mount of Olives
and another in Bethlehem, and is supposed to have discovered the True Cross. She appears with Constantine in
a mosaic as late as the 17th century, in S. Marco in Venice.

St. John Chrysostom (347–407), the "golden-mouthed," so-called on
account of his rhetorical abilities; once a hermit and later
patriarch of Constantinople. Through his bluntness he got
into difficulties, and was exiled to Antioch, where he died
of the rough treatment he received. He is famous for his
sermons and his clear theological and moral thinking.

St. Julitta, a female saint (d. 303), appears in Monreale, Sicily, and
in S. Maria Antiqua in Rome.

St. Methodius (815–85) was associated with his brother Cyril in his
missionary work in Moravia.

St. Nicholas (d. 350), Bishop of Myra in Lycia, one of the most
popular Greek saints but also much venerated in the West.
He is said to have been imprisoned by Diocletian but afterwards released. He is known for his good deeds. Justinian
built the first church known to be dedicated to him, the
church of St. Priscus and St. Nicholas, in Constantinople.
The popularity of St. Nicholas caused the sailors of Bari to
cross over to Myra to capture his remains from the infidel

[ON OPPOSITE PAGE] *Portable mosaic with
feasts of the church (Opera del Duomo, Florence)*

and rebury them in their native town, where they have since rested. The kindly face of St. Nicholas with his small mouth, appearing so often on icons and frescoes, is bound to become familiar to the Byzantine traveller.

St. Nilus of Rossano (d. 1005), after living as a hermit and a monk, became abbot of S. Adriano near S. Demetrio Corone (p. 99), which he left on account of the raids of the Saracens, and later founded the monastery of Grottaferrata (p. 71).

St. Pantaleon, or Panteleimon (d. ca. 305) was, according to legend, a physician to Diocletian; when Panteleimon became converted to Christianity, the emperor martyred him for his faith.

St. Paul of Thebes (d. ca. 340), a desert saint. It is said that St. Antony visited him when St. Paul was 113 years old and buried him when he died (for the meeting of the two saints, see S. Angelo in Formis, p. 82). St. Paul is often depicted beside a palm tree, as in S. Angelo in Formis. Two great monasteries, St. Paul and St. Antony, in the desert near the Gulf of Suez in Egypt, are named after these two famous saints.

St. Susanna (d. 295), martyred for refusing to marry a prince, appears in Monreale.

St. Thecla, converted to Christianity by St. Paul in Iconium (Konya, in Asia Minor) and martyred in the first century, appears in both Monreale and Poreč.

St. Theodore Tiro (d. 306), soldier martyr, often appears with a dragon or crocodile at his feet, as we see him on his column on the Piazzetta in Venice, where he preceded St. Mark as patron saint of the city.

Finally, the use of Greek lettering in many monuments in Italy shows clearly their relation to the East.

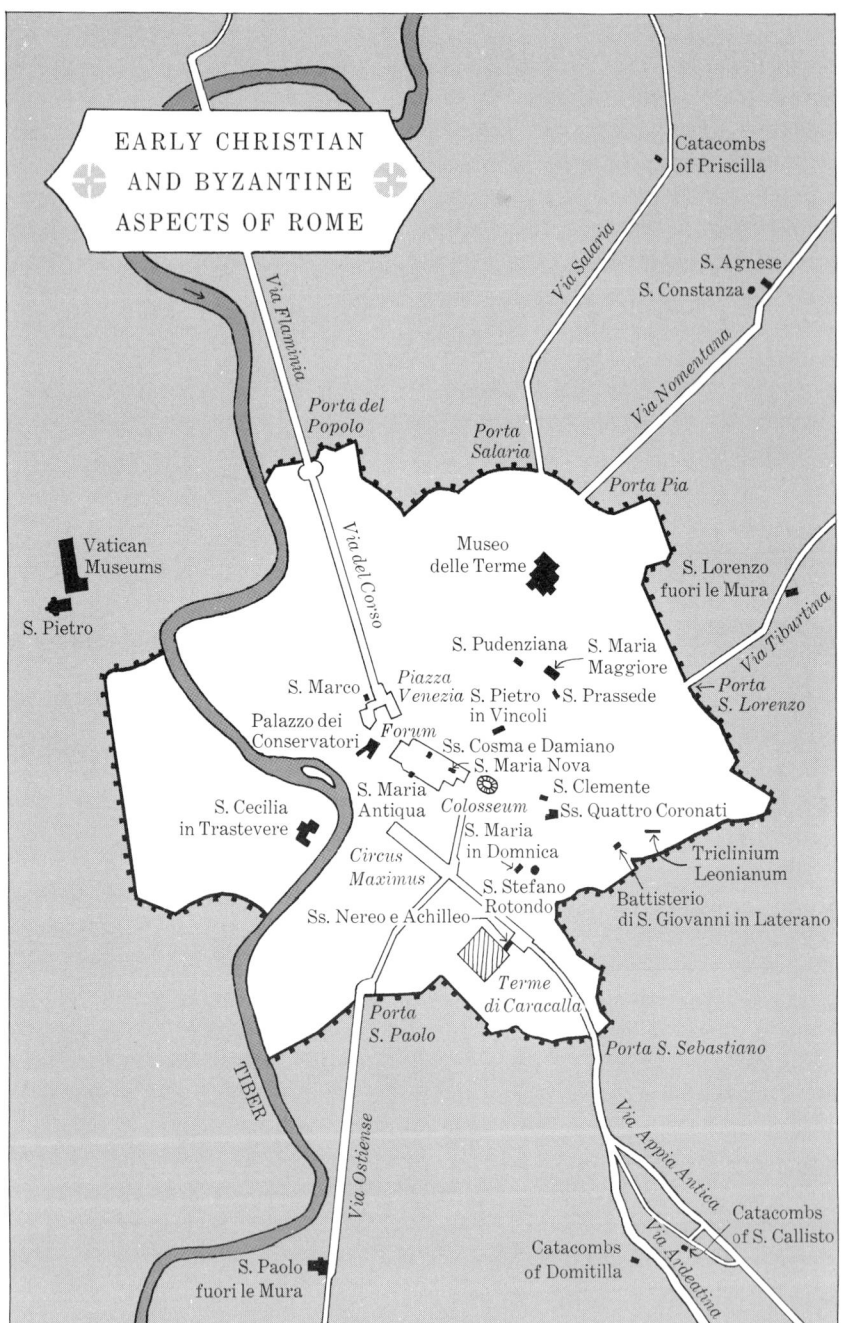

EARLY CHRISTIAN
AND BYZANTINE
ASPECTS OF ROME

Catacombs
of Priscilla

Via Salaria

S. Agnese
S. Constanza

Via Nomentana

Via Flaminia

*Porta del
Popolo*

*Porta
Salaria*

Porta Pia

Vatican
Museums

Museo
delle Terme

S. Lorenzo
fuori le Mura

Via Tiburtina

S. Pietro

S. Pudenziana   S. Maria
Maggiore

←*Porta
S. Lorenzo*

S. Marco   *Piazza
Venezia*   S. Pietro   ◆S. Prassede
in Vincoli

Palazzo dei
Conservatori   *Forum*   Ss. Cosma e Damiano

S. Maria Nova

S. Maria   S. Clemente
Antiqua   *Colosseum*   Ss. Quattro Coronati

S. Cecilia
in Trastevere

S. Maria   Triclinium
in Domnica   Leonianum

*Circus
Maximus*

S. Stefano
Rotondo

Ss. Nereo e Achilleo   Battisterio
di S. Giovanni in Laterano

*Porta
S. Paolo*

*Terme
di Caracalla*

Porta S. Sebastiano

TIBER

Via Appia Antica

Catacombs
of S. Callisto

Via Ostiense

Via Ardeatina

Catacombs
of Domitilla

S. Paolo
fuori le Mura

III

EARLY CHRISTIAN AND BYZANTINE ASPECTS OF ROME

EXAMPLES of Byzantine aspects of Rome are spread over various periods of the city's history. The formative period is represented in the great number of monuments from the "underground" times of budding Christianity and its subsequent open development. These include the frescoes of the catacombs, the sculptures of the sarcophagi, and small objects from the catacombs, excellent examples of which are exhibited in the Museo Sacro of the Vatican.

A further step in the growth of a new style is evident in early Christian wall mosaics, which, partly under influences from the East, begin to free themselves from the classic style. Good examples are the 4th-century mosaics of the Rotunda of S. Costanza; the 4th/5th-century apse mosaic of S. Pudenziana; and the middle-5th-century mosaics in S. Maria Maggiore, which were set up by

Pope Sixtus III (432–40) after the Council of Ephesus (p. 20) where East and West cooperated, and which include among their subjects the veneration of the Virgin.

Greek influence in Rome grew after this. Eastern Orthodox fled the Middle East and North Africa to escape the sudden Arab explosion. In the 7th and early 8th centuries, half the popes came from the East. The number of pious Orthodox increased through iconodules who sought refuge in Rome from persecution by iconoclastic Byzantium. The northeast side of the Palatine, in the region of the Forum Romanum, became a Greek center.

Many churches show examples of this Eastern background. We see it in the mosaic of the triumphal arch of S. Lorenzo fuori le Mura set up by Pope Pelagius II (578–90), and in the apse mosaic of S. Agnese fuori le Mura set up by Pope Honorius I (625–38).

S. Maria Antiqua (p. 55), situated in the Greek Palatine center, shows an abundance of Eastern influence, and Ss. Nereo e Achilleo has above the apse the Eastern-oriented mosaic, set up by Pope Leo III (795–816), of the Transfiguration, a favorite Eastern theme.

All the three churches built or rebuilt by Pope Paschal (817–24)—S. Cecilia in Trastevere, S. Prassede, and S. Maria in Domnica —have mosaics of his time influenced by the East. The same holds for S. Marco, rebuilt by Pope Gregory IV (828–44). The 8th/9th-century frescoes in the lower church of S. Clemente are also Byzantine-inspired.

Even when Constantinople had been occupied by the Fourth Crusade, Byzantine style came to Rome indirectly when Venetian mosaicists still working in the Byzantine tradition set up the apse mosaic in S. Paolo fuori le Mura. In 1246 also, such artisans painted the frescoes in the church of the Ss. Quattro Coronati.

We meet Byzantium, too, in the 6th/7th-century encaustic icon (probably imported) of S. Maria Nova and in the mosaic of St. Sebastian in S. Pietro in Vincoli, to name but a couple of examples.

In nearby Grottaferrata, some 30 km. southeast of Rome, where Byzantine rites still prevail, the 11th/13th-century mosaics with their Greek inscriptions were doubtlessly set up by artisans still working in Byzantine traditions.

CATACOMBS

ONE MAY, in looking at the early Christian frescoes in the Roman catacombs, criticize them for their often crude aspect. Yet one must remember that such paintings, which besides are often quite faded, were not made primarily for artistic purposes, and also that they were executed at a time when the classic style was decaying. Some remnants of the classic style, indeed, are to be seen, transitional between the classic and the new Christian styles that were gradually appearing also in the early wall mosaics.

The early images in the catacomb frescoes as well as in the sculpture of the Christian sarcophagi, though Christian in character, do not present Christian subjects openly. Nowhere is Christ himself shown at first, only his symbol, the fish. The scenes, frequently ornamented with the peacocks and grapes that symbolize eternal life, are mostly taken from the Old Testament but gradually come to include cryptic Christian and, finally, openly Christian subjects from the New Testament and representations of Christ himself. For a summary of these the reader is referred to Chapter II above.

There are a great many catacombs in Rome but only a few are normally open to the public. Though authorization to visit the others may be applied for, it may take some time to make arrangements. From seeing three that are open to the public—those of S. Domitilla, S. Callisto, and Priscilla—one will derive a fair, if far from complete, impression of catacomb paintings.

Catacombs of S. Domitilla */Via delle Sette Chiese, near Via Ardeatina/* On descending into the catacombs one comes to the ruined Basilica of Ss. Nereo e Achilleo (either slaves of Domitilla or military saints [*]), to the left of which one passes into the Ipogeo dei Flavii, the burial ground of the family of that name. Near the entrance is a fresco of Eros and Psyche, Pompeian style, dated by some around 200, by others around 100. Close by, in niches of a gallery, are some crypto-Christian pictures symbolizing eternal life:

[*] An epitaph in the catacomb seems to support the latter theory, saying: "They entered military service and both practiced their cruel trade, carrying out the commands of the tyrant prepared, out of fear, to accomplish his orders. Then behold a visible miracle . . ." (quoted in F. van der Meer, *The Atlas of the Early Christian World,* London, 1958, p. 147).

Daniel in the lions' den, fishermen, the Good Shepherd (2nd century); and also, in the Cripta di Ampliato, frescoes of the 3rd and 4th centuries openly showing Christian images: the Virgin with Christ child, the four Magi, Christ and Apostles.

In a chapel behind the basilica is a 4th-century fresco of the martyr St. Petronilla (venerated in the basilica with Sts. Nereus and Achilleus) conducting the deceased lady (called Veneranda) into the garden of Paradise.

Catacombs of S. Callisto /On road to catacombs branching off from Via Appia Antica at church of Domine Quo Vadis/ These catacombs contain, among many other things, near the entrance the Crypt of the Popes in which several 3rd-century popes, martyred during the persecution of the Christians, were buried.

Near the Crypt of the Popes is the Crypt of S. Cecilia, with frescoes (6th/7th century) that may have been influenced by the East. Here we see the martyr represented as young and elegant, dressed richly with embroidery and precious stones, looking like a Byzantine princess. Above her is a fresco of Christ, and under it, to the right, one of Pope Urban (222–30), both probably of the same period as the fresco of St. Cecilia.

Several sacramental chapels in the catacombs (all but the first, where there is nothing left) show interesting frescoes, all of the 3rd century. Among these:

IN CHAPEL A-2: A baptism (back wall), a Good Shepherd (in vault), Jonah resting, Lazarus resurrected, a fisherman, Moses striking water from the rock, the banquet of the seven disciples at the Sea of Tiberias.

IN A-3: Traces, much faded, of a Good Shepherd (in vault), the Living Water, a fisherman, John the Baptist baptizing Christ (faint traces of the Dove above), the paralytic healed taking up his bed and walking, the Food of Life (bread and fish on a small table) with an *orans* and a youthful figure (Christ?), the multiplication of loaves and fishes, Abraham and Isaac praying.

IN A-4: A Good Shepherd (in vault), a much-faded cycle of Jonah, and other barely recognizable scenes.

IN A-5: Jonah resting, banquet of the seven disciples at the Sea of Tiberias.

IN A-6: The Living Water, resurrection of Lazarus, a Jonah cycle, and again the seven disciples at table with loaves and fishes.

In the Chapel of Pope Miltiades (310–14) stands a sarcophagus showing Christ as the Good Shepherd and the resurrection of Lazarus.

The Crypt of Lucina is the oldest part of the S. Callisto catacombs. It consists of two connecting rooms with frescoes of the 2nd century. The first shows Christ after his baptism being helped out of the water by John the Baptist, the Dove of the Holy Spirit above, and, left and right of the door to the second chamber, two saints. In the vault of the second chamber: Daniel in the lions' den, two Good Shepherds, and two *orantes,* the oldest known; further, the history of Jonah, and, on each side wall, a fish with a basket of bread through the fabric of which one sees a flask of wine—clearly an early representation of the Eucharist.

Catacombs of Priscilla */On Via Salaria, just beyond Piazza di Priscilla/* These catacombs, probably constructed in the 2nd century though the frescoes may be later, are among the most important in Rome. The so-called Cappella Greca, or funeral-meal chamber, has especially interesting frescoes, among them the three youths in the fiery furnace, Noah *orans,* the sacrifice of Abraham, Moses striking the rock for water (above the entrance), Susanna with the Elders and Daniel (side wall), the Magi offering their gifts (above niche in main wall), the Celestial Banquet, Noah in the ark.

In another crypt, that of the Velatio Virginis (Veiling of the Virgin), there is a fresco of the Prophecy of Isaiah (Isa. 7:14), a subject not often represented.

Catacombs of Priscilla:
Virgin with Child, in the crypt of
the Velatio Virginis (a very early
appearance of this subject)

SARCOPHAGI

NEXT TO THE FRESCOES of the catacombs, the Christian sarcophagi are the best sources for study of the developing Christian art. They are generally well preserved and give the visitor an excellent perspective of the evolution of the Christian motives described in Chapter II, *Concerning Iconography.*

The Museo Christiano of the Lateran, which has a big collection of sarcophagi, has unfortunately been closed and its treasures, to be transferred to the Vatican, are not open to the public at this writing. There are other sources, however:

• I *Aula III of the Museo Nazionale Romano e delle Terme* (in the ruins of the Baths of Diocletian, on the Piazza della Repubblica) has a number of Christian sarcophagi of great interest, often showing biblical scenes among their decorative ornamentation.

Of those placed along the left wall of the room as one enters, the first includes: the multiplication of the loaves, the marriage at Cana, the healing of the blind, the woman with the issue of blood; the second, Jesus as teacher; the third, two drinking glasses (Eucharist?); the fourth, an *orans,* and left, Moses striking the rock, right, the Good Shepherd.

Of those along the back wall, the first shows: the resurrection of Lazarus, Jesus healing the blind, the multiplication of the loaves, the entry into Jerusalem, the marriage at Cana, the healing of the paralytic, Moses striking the rock; the second (center of back wall): Moses striking the rock, the capture of Peter, the marriage at Cana, the multiplication of the loaves, the healing of the blind, the denial of Peter, the resurrection of Lazarus; the third: Moses striking the rock, the capture of Peter, Abraham offering his son, the Virgin *orans,* the miracle of the man born blind, the resurrection of Lazarus; above these pictures also the Magi (right) and Jonah (left).

Against the right wall there is only one sarcophagus: on its cover, Jonah, and the multiplication of the loaves, and below, a defunct and a pastoral scene.

Against the entrance wall, left of the door, a sarcophagus showing Christ as teacher with two disciples, and left and right, a remnant of the classical time, Amor and Psyche.

• II *In the Museo del Palazzo dei Conservatori* (on the Campidoglio), near the head of the staircase are two rooms of Christian monuments, among them sarcophagi repeatedly showing biblical scenes: the Good Shepherd (of which there is also a 3rd-century statuette), the resurrection of Lazarus, the sacrifice of Abraham, and various *orantes.* Noteworthy also, in Room II, is a 5th/6th-century statue (traditionally called Amalasuntha, Theodoric's daughter and regent for the Gothic king Athalaric, 526–34), the head of which is that of a Byzantine empress.

• III *The Sala a Croce Greca* in the Museo Pio-Clementino in the Vatican has two beautiful 4th-century porphyry sarcophagi, one of St. Costanza, Constantine's daughter, the other of St. Helena, his famous mother. The former is generally considered to be the one that stood in the Rotunda of S. Costanza. Among its decorations it shows peacocks and wine-harvesting putti, both possibly symbols of eternal life. The second sarcophagus is decorated with lively secular scenes in classic style.

CHURCH MOSAICS AND FRESCOES

IN ORDER TO FACILITATE study of the development of style during the centuries, the churches are here discussed, as far as possible, according to the chronological sequence of the dates of origin of their oldest mosaics or frescoes. Travelers wishing to visit the monuments in a geographically convenient sequence may find the map (p. 42) helpful in arranging an itinerary.

The Rotunda of S. Costanza /Via Nomentana, next to S. Agnese fuori le Mura/ The Rotunda of S. Costanza, which became a baptistery in the 5th century, was built as a mausoleum for the daughters of Constantine the Great, Costanza and Helena, and is supposed to have originally contained Costanza's porphyry sarcophagus (now in the Vatican). The building is of the 4th century, and its mosaics, among the oldest ceiling mosaics known, are of the same period. Besides purely decorative motifs, they include medallions, birds, pitchers and other objects, and wine-making scenes with putti, similar to those on the sarcophagus of Costanza; also two portraits that could well be the portraits of St. Costanza and her husband Hannibalianus.

S. Costanza: ceiling mosaic

Below, *Christ handing key to St. Peter*

The mosaics are considered to have Eastern features, comparable, according to Charles Diehl (*Histoire de l'art byzantin*), to the hunting scenes in the mosaics of Kabr-Hiram in the Lebanon. One may also recall in this connection the floor mosaics of Piazza Armerina in Sicily, which show oriental aspects in their hunting scenes (p. 142), and furthermore the later (5th-century) decorative mosaics in the church of St. George in Salonika in Northern Greece, with their birds, fruits, etc.

Two niches in the Rotunda contain mosaics considered to be either 4th/5th- or 5th/6th-century, with openly Christian subjects. One shows Christ seated on a globe (compare the mosaic above the apse in Poreč, first half of 6th century), giving the key to St. Peter; and the other, Christ standing between St. Peter and St. Paul, handing over the law (*traditio legis*) to the former.

S. Pudenziana /*Via Urbana, very near the east side of* S. *Maria Maggiore*/ The church may have been built on the site of the house of the senator Pudens, who according to tradition offered hospitality to St. Peter. The house later gave place to a

S. Pudenziana: apse mosaic

thermal bath, which in its turn was transformed, around the 4th/ 5th centuries into the basilica dedicated to St. Pudentiana, sister of St. Praxedes (p. 64). The apse mosaic is of this latter period.

The mosaic as we see it now has been heavily restored and cut. It shows Christ as teacher, seated and holding in his hand a book bearing the words "Dominus Conservator Ecclesiae Pudentianae"; at each side, five disciples, seated; behind Christ, a symbolic panorama of Jerusalem; above, the Cross; in the sky, the symbols of the Evangelists (Ezek. 1:10 and Rev. 4:7). The lion of St. Mark and the ox of St. Luke have been nearly fully conserved; of the man of St. Matthew and the eagle of St. John, only tiny bits remain. It is obvious that a large part of the mosaic has been lost, which accounts for the disappearance of the greater part of the symbols of St. Matthew and St. John and of two of the twelve Disciples.

Behind the Disciples are two women, each with a wreath in her hands, one crowning St. Paul, the other St. Peter. While according to some the two women, though they do not wear haloes, may be St. Pudentiana and St. Praxedes, they may rather represent the two churches from which the primitive Christian congregations were recruited; one often encounters representations in which the Jewish element (ecclesia ex circumcisione) crowns Peter as its recognized head and symbol, while the other, the gentile element (ecclesia ex gentibus) crowns Paul.

The restorations and cuttings have certainly harmed the mosaic a great deal. Yet it has the interesting features of the period of its production, such as the teacher version of Christ. The appearance of Jerusalem in the background is also noteworthy, seeming to foreshadow the pictures of Jerusalem and Bethlehem so familiar in subsequent mosaics.

Back of the church is the Oratorio Mariano, which has a number of interesting 11th-century frescoes. The fresco above the altar, of the Virgin between St. Pudentiana and St. Praxedes, shows Byzantine features.

S. Maria Maggiore /Piazza S. Maria Maggiore/ Pope Sixtus III (432–40) rebuilt a secular building into the present (though at various times restored and reconstructed) S. Maria Maggiore. This was after the ecumenical council of Ephesus (431) had approved the title of Theotokos ("God-Bearer," or as one

mostly sees it on icons or mosaics, *Mater Theou,* "Mother of God"),
sanctioning the cult of the Virgin Mary that has brought us so
many beautiful mosaics, frescoes, and icons. The building of S.
Maria Maggiore thus became the first manifestation of the new
doctrine.

The church was successor to an older church that Pope Liberius
(352–66) had founded, probably near the present structure, after
a vision on a snowy day in summer. It is therefore sometimes called
S. Maria della Neve (of the Snow) or S. Maria Liberiana, after
Pope Liberius. Behind the new 18th-century facade of the present
basilica, on the rear wall of the loggia that was the original facade
of Pope Sixtus' building, there are (in an area closed to the public) 13th-century mosaics, one of which pictures the vision of
Pope Liberius.

Of the mosaics inside the church, both those on the triumphal
arch and those high up along both sides of the nave, with their
Old Testament subjects, are of the period of Pope Sixtus.

The mosaics in the apse, which replaced the original apse of
Pope Sixtus, were set up in 1296. Under the original mosaic was
an inscription beginning "Mary Virgin, to thee I Sixtus dedicate
this new abode."

• *Triumphal Arch.* Though the old apse mosaic has
disappeared, the Sixtus mosaic of the triumphal arch shows clearly
enough his original purpose in building the church. Above the
arch we find the throne of Christ, before it Peter (left) and Paul
(right) and below it the name of Pope Sixtus (*Kystus Episcopus
plebi Dei*). The subjects presented on the arch are much debated,
but the following may give an acceptable description:

UPPER ZONE, *from left to right:* Annunciation, Presentation in the
   Temple, Flight into Egypt. The Annunciation follows here
   the Eastern version with the Virgin spinning purple wool
   (see p. 35) as we see it in the church of Justinian's time
   at Poreć.

SECOND ZONE: *left,* Adoration of the Magi;
   right, Christ's disputation with the doctors.

THIRD ZONE: *left,* Massacre of the Innocents;
   right, the Magi before Herod.

FOURTH ZONE: *left,* Jerusalem;
   right, Bethlehem.

• *Apse.* On the arch of the apse, above, the Lamb; at the sides, elders offering crowns, above them symbols of the Evangelists.

The apse mosaic (13th/14th centuries) shows Christ enthroned *with* his mother—a most unusual form; at each side nine angels, and left, Sts. Peter, Paul, and Francis; under them (smaller) to their right, Pope Nicolas IV (1288–92) as donor; right, Sts. John the Baptist, John the Evangelist, and Antony; under them (smaller) Cardinal Colonna. Between the windows: Death of the Virgin, Annunciation, Nativity, Purification (Presentation in the Temple), Epiphany. All these motives are Eastern in their presentation.

• *Nave.* The nave mosaics are not easy to study since they are placed high and poorly lighted. To see them better, one may ask at the sacristy to have them lighted (payment required).

Many of these mosaics have been restored, and some have been replaced by frescoes. The pictures are so numerous that instead of identifying them one by one we here list some of the subjects, giving the relevant Bible references and indicating further biblical texts that cover the development of the stories.

Starting from the altar, the left (north) wall shows: The offering of Melchisedec (Gen. 14:18); the hospitality of Abraham (Gen. 18:2); the partition of territory between Abraham and Lot (Gen. 13:11–12); Isaac blessing Jacob, believing he blesses Esau (Gen. 27:23). The stories then continue of Esau, Jacob, Rachel and Leah, Laban, Jacob's return to his own country, as told in Gen. 27:30; 29:13, 18, 20, and 28; 30:32–36; 31:3–4; and, further, the stories of Jacob, and of Hamor and Schechem (Gen. 34:6–7, 13–14).

Returning to the altar and following thence along the right (south) wall we see episodes of the lives of Moses and Joshua: the adoption of Moses by Pharaoh's daughter (Exod. 2:10); the marriage of Moses (Exod. 2:21); the vision of the burning bush (Exod. 3:2); the passage through the Red Sea (Exod. 14:21); followed by further events as told in Exod. 15:24–25; 16:13; 17:6, 8 and 10–16, and in Num. 13:26–33 and chap. 15; then Exodus again (35:1), ending with the death of Moses (as told in Deut. 34:5) and the Ark of the Covenant (Deut. 10:8). There follows further the story of Joshua as told in his book: 2:1, 23–24; 3:14–17; 5:13–15; 6:1–24; 9:15, 26; 10:12–13, 23–27.

S. Maria Antiqua /*On the Forum Romanum, entrance to the southeast of the Temple of Castor and Pollux*/ S. Maria Antiqua, situated in the Forum, was founded in the beginning of the 6th century by Greek monks who transformed a pagan building in the Greek center around the Palatine into a church. Many Byzantine officials lived in this area, and it is natural that the decoration of the church should convey a strong Greek influence by the selection of Eastern saints and subjects in its iconography.

Unfortunately the frescoes are rapidly fading, and many have become hardly recognizable. Yet what remains is interesting enough and instructive—indeed, a must—for the Byzantine-oriented traveller as an example of Greek influence on art in Rome. As Grabar says (*La Peinture byzantine*, p. 80), though not all the frescoes are Byzantine, the origin of many of them certainly is, especially that of the 7th- and 8th-century pictures in the church; except for the deterioration that has taken place since the discovery of the church (only some 65 years ago now), S. Maria Antiqua would be "a real museum of Byzantine art contemporary with the iconoclastic period." Later frescoes are often superimposed upon earlier pictures, as may be seen in cases where the various layers can be distinguished. In the sanctuary of the church the palimpsest wall (as it is called, after the vellum or papyrus material from which a previous text was erased to make further use possible) has no less than five layers, each of a different period.

• *Atrium.* The atrium before the church is a construction of the period of Domitian (81–96). Just inside the entrance, to the left, there is a small fresco of a female saint with some Greek lettering. On the left wall, under a protecting roof, is a fresco of the oriental doctor saint Abbacyr, dated 7th/8th century. From the right wall a big fresco has obviously been removed.

• *Inside the Church.* On entering the church we find this fresco relocated in the right aisle. It represents the Virgin enthroned among saints and angels, and includes a portrait of Pope Adrian I (772–95) with the square nimbus of the living, which dates the picture. In a niche to its right is a fresco of the Virgin between Anna, her mother, and Elisabeth, mother of John the Baptist. Each of the three has her own child in her lap. Right of the entrance, in a little niche in a pier, is a Madonna and Child and on the opposite pier a fresco of a single figure.

Along the wall of the left aisle are a number of pagan and Christian sarcophagi, the wall itself bearing elaborate frescoes in three superimposed rows. The two upper rows show Old Testament scenes. The uppermost is very much damaged. The middle row shows such scenes as Jacob's dream, Jacob's struggle with the angel, Joseph taken out of the cistern and sold by his brothers, Joseph and Potiphar's wife, and Joseph being taken to prison. The lowest shows Christ seated in the center of a row of saints, those to his right belonging to the West, those to his left to the East. The frescoes are probably 7th-century. The Greek lettering should be noted.

Of the two piers just before one enters the presbytery, the left shows an Annunciation, dated 7th century. On the right pier is the fresco of Salomona and her seven sons, the Maccabee martyrs, with the scribe Eleazar, who all died for their belief (see Chapter II, p. 33). The fresco probably dates from the reign of Pope Martin I (649–53).

Just behind this pier, on a wall to the right, we see King Hezekiah on his deathbed, with the prophet Isaiah (II Kings 20:1–11 and Isaiah 38:1–8).

S. Maria Antiqua: Salomona

• *Presbytery.* Above the apse: Exaltation of the Cross, with angels (to the right, an old man—John the Baptist?). In the apse: Christ blessing, with Virgin and donor Pope Paul I (757–67) with the square halo of the living. All these are very much spoiled.

To the right of the apse we find the palimpsest wall previously mentioned, with its five layers from different periods:

FIRST LAYER (6th century): a crowned Madonna (upper left), looking very Byzantine, with Christ child and adored by angels.

SECOND LAYER (first half of 7th century): Annunciation. Only part of the Virgin (upper center) and the head of the angel to the right above her are preserved.

THIRD LAYER (middle of 7th century): below the Madonnas, heads of two church fathers who were cited at the Lateran Council of 649.

FOURTH LAYER (early 8th century): head of a church father (to the right of the head of the crowned Madonna), the only one remaining of another row of church fathers added by Pope John VII (705–07), who decorated the whole sanctuary.

FIFTH LAYER: containing the remaining frescoes, was added by Pope Paul I.

• *Chapel of Ss. Quirico e Giulitta.* On the left side of the presbytery, the Chapel of Ss. Quirico e Giulitta shows a well-preserved 8th-century Crucifixion in the Eastern style of that subject: far left and right, the Madonna and St. John; near Christ, left, Longinus piercing His side with a spear (John XIX:34) and right, a man (Stephaton?) giving Him, on a reed, the sponge filled with vinegar (Matt. 27:48).

The fresco formerly under that of the Crucifixion has been taken from the wall and is now in the Antiquarium Forense or Museo del Foro, near the Arch of Titus on the Forum. It shows the Virgin with, on the left, St. Peter, St. Julitta, Pope Zacharias (741–52) with square nimbus, and on the right, St. Paul and St. Quiricus. Theodotus, its administrator, offers the church bearing the motto: "Sancta Maria quae vocatur Antiqua."

The left and right walls of the chapel depict the martyrdom of St. Julitta, the right-hand side of the right wall showing Theodotus with his wife, son, and daughter.

The inside of the entrance wall (as one leaves the chapel) shows left, Theodotus asking the protection of Sts. Julitta and Quiricus, and right, four unknown saints.

Baptistery of S. Giovanni in Laterano */Piazza S. Giovanni in Laterano/* At the back of S. Giovanni in Laterano lies the Baptistery (at date of writing, closed for repairs), founded by Constantine, first restored by Pope Sixtus III (432–40) in the middle of the 5th century, and again restored and very much changed in 1637 by Pope Urban VIII. One enters it through bronze doors. In an apsidiole at left is a 5th-century mosaic.

In the Chapel of S. Venanzio (a Dalmatian martyr), founded by Pope John IV in 640, there are mosaics of the 7th century: above the arch, symbols of the Evangelists; at the sides, Jerusalem and Bethlehem, and below, the eight martyrs of Salona (in Dalmatia); in a niche, Christ giving his benediction between two angels, and below, the Virgin with six saints and the Popes John IV (640–42) and Theodore I (642–49).

The Chapel of S. Giovanni Evangelista has 5th-century mosaic decorations of birds and flowers in the vault.

Ss. Cosma e Damiano */Via dei Fori Imperiali, alongside the Forum Romanum/* This 6th-century church, combining two buildings on the Forum Romanum, was founded by Pope Felix IV (526–30)—that is to say, before Justinian had recaptured Italy from the barbarians and at a time when there was hardly any contact with the East. The mosaics, set up at about the same time as the church itself, show Sts. Cosmas and Damian, those two penniless physicians who always refused to be paid for their services, together with St. Theodore Tiro, the oriental soldier-martyr (see p. 40). Diehl (*Justinian*, p. 607) calls them the last effort of an original invention, and adds that though the plan of the church reminds one of the East and though the chosen saints were especially dear to the East, the art of Ss. Cosma e Damiano is still Roman and "owes nothing to the lessons of Byzantium," whereas the mosaics of the triumphal arch in S. Lorenzo fuori le Mura (p. 61), restored under Pope Pelagius II (578–90) and dating only 50 years later, are quite Eastern.

Oddly enough, the Roman pattern of the mosaics of Ss. Cosma e Damiano served as prototype for the mosaics of four subsequent churches in which Greek influence prevails. Hence it is important to visit this Roman church before seeing the Eastern-style mosaics in the four churches in question. Three of these—S. Cecilia in

Trastevere, S. Prassede, and S. Maria in Domnica—were built by Pope Paschal I (817–24), and the fourth, S. Marco, by Pope Gregory IV (828–44; see p. 44).

The church of Ss. Cosma e Damiano was much restored in 1632, and the mosaics suffered severe losses by the cutting away of part of the surface.

On the arch above the apse we see, in a medallion: center, the Lamb of God on the throne (Rev. 5:6); beside the throne, seven candlesticks (the seven lamps of fire, Rev. 4:5); left and right of these, at each side, two angels; far left, the angel (man) with book, the symbol of St. Matthew; and far right, the eagle of St. John. The symbols of St. Mark and St. Luke were cut off in the above-mentioned renovation, while of the 24 elders (Rev. 4:4) holding wreaths, in the spandrels left and right below, only two hands with wreaths have survived.

Ss. Cosma e Damiano: right side of mosaic on arch of apse

Ss. Cosma e Damiano: apse mosaic

The mosaic in the apse itself shows: center, Christ standing on a pathway of clouds, above him the hand of God holding a wreath to crown him, below him the river Jordan. Left of Christ, St. Paul introducing Cosmas, and at right, St. Peter introducing Damian with his red medicine case. Far left and right, a palm tree, in the left one the bird of paradise, symbol of immortality. Next to the palm tree, left, Pope Felix IV, the donor, with the model of the church, and right, St. Theodore Tiro.

Under this mosaic, the Lamb, standing on the mount from which flow the four rivers of Paradise, with six lambs coming from Jerusalem and Bethlehem, representing respectively the church of the Jews and the church of the Gentiles.

S. Lorenzo fuori le Mura */Piazzale di* S. *Lorenzo/* This church in its present form is a strange construction of two churches built back to back. The old one, with which we are concerned, is a totally reconstructed building of the time of Pope Pelagius II (578–90) on the site of the original church built by Constantine where the mortuary chapel of S. Lorenzo stood. The later church, of the time of Pope Honorius III (1216–27), was severely bombed in 1944 and afterwards rebuilt. One first enters this church and finds one's way through it to the old church of Pelagius.

The mosaic on the triumphal arch in this old church is, like the the church itself, of the 6th century. One is immediately struck by the difference in style with the great mosaic of Ss. Cosma e Damiano only some 50 years older—but Roman, while this is Eastern. It shows Christ, center, seated on a globe; to the right, St. Paul with Sts. Stephen and Hippolytus; to the left, St. Peter and St. Lawrence presenting Pope Pelagius, who bears the model of the church. Further down, at the sides, the towns of Bethlehem and Jerusalem. The mosaic has been much restored.

S. Agnese: detail of apse mosaic

S. Agnese fuori le Mura /*Via Nomentana, corner of Via di S. Agnese*/ The church of S. Agnese was restored by Pope Symmachus (498–514). The mosaic decoration in the apse dates from 625–40; its execution was ordered by Pope Honorius I (625–38). The composition differs from those of both Ss. Cosma e Damiano and S. Lorenzo fuori le Mura. Instead of Christ, St. Agnes is the central figure in the mosaic. St. Agnes, condemned to be burned, passed unhurt through the fire (note the flames below her), only to be decapitated. The sword with which the deed was done (in 304) lies at her feet. The saint is dressed as a Byzantine empress wearing costly clothes and precious stones, on her head a golden crown. The whole picture is simple. Only two persons appear in the entourage, Popes Symmachus and Honorius; Pope Symmachus (left) carries the model of the church he restored.

S. Stefano Rotondo /*Via di S. Stefano Rotondo, on the Caelian Hill*/ The rotunda may have been erected in the 4th century by Galla Placidia, daughter of the Roman emperor Theodosius the Great (379–95), who built the famous mausoleum in Ravenna, and who may have wished to reproduce in Rome the church her grandmother Eudoxia had built in Jerusalem in honor of St. Stephen.

Another view holds that it was built by Pope Simplicius (468–83) and should accordingly be dated 5th century. Its style is related to the East. It originally had two rings of columns, but in the rebuilding by Pope Nicolas V in 1453 the outer row unfortunately was removed. The inner row of columns carries a wall with occasional windows.

The apse mosaic in the chapel to the left of the entrance shows a cross supporting a bust of Christ, above his head the Hand of God with a wreath, left and right Sts. Primus and Felician. Morey (*Early Christian Art*) considers that the remains of the saints were transferred to the Rotunda by Pope Theodore I (642–49) from their original burying place in the Via Nomentana and hence assumes that this pope should also be credited with the mosaic, especially as the rendering of a bust of Christ above a cross is a Palestinian form, and Pope Theodore himself came from Palestine.

Ss. Nereo e Achilleo /*Between the Via delle Terme di Caracalla and the Terme themselves*/ This church is mentioned as

Ss. Nereo e Achilleo: right side of mosaic on arch of apse

early as the first half of the 5th century. It was renovated around the year 800 by Pope Leo III (794–806), in whose time the mosaic of the Transfiguration on the arch over the apse was set up.

The Transfiguration—when Christ, flanked by Moses and Elijah, appeared in the heavenly light to the disciples Peter, John, and James—is a theme dear to the Eastern church. It is the subject of many icons, but is rarely seen on the arch over the apse; in the Church of St. Catherine on Mt. Sinai it is placed in the apse itself.

Here the mosaic shows Christ in the center of the arch, with Elijah to the left and Moses to the right, both standing; further left, Peter and James, further right, John, all kneeling; left corner, the Annunciation; right corner, the Virgin with the Christ child and an angel. Over the arch, in Latin, the famous text of St. Luke (9:35): "This is my beloved Son: hear him."

S. Cecilia in Trastevere /*Via di S. Cecilia*/ The original church is 5th-century but was rebuilt by Pope Paschal I (817–24) who, having received a revelation that the bones of St. Cecilia were buried in the catacombs of S. Callisto (p. 46), caused them to be reburied in this church in 821. Like the mosaics in the other two churches he built (see below), these are strongly influenced by the East.

Here the great apse mosaic shows us Christ in the attitude of blessing *alla greca;* left, St. Paul, St. Agatha, and Paschal I (with square halo) holding the usual model of the church; right, Sts. Peter, Valerius, and Cecilia; below, the Lamb and the cities of Jerusalem and Bethlehem.

S. Prassede */in Via S. Martino ai Monti, the second small side-street on the right of the Via Merulana after leaving Piazza S. Maria Maggiore/* This church was built by Pope Paschal I in 822. The mosaics of the triumphal arch, the apse, and the Chapel of S. Zenone are all of his time. Those of the triumphal arch and apse, like those in the churches of S. Cecilia in Trastevere, S. Maria in Domnica, and S. Marco, though based on the Roman pattern of Ss. Cosma e Damiano, show the prevailing Greek stylistic influence of their period.

The triumphal arch shows Christ between two angels, under them Sts. Praxedes and Pudentiana with the Elected of the Lord, and, at the sides, Pudens and Sts. Timothy and Novatius; at one end, New Jerusalem, and at the other, guardian angels; under the arch, the monogram of Pope Paschal.

On the arch surrounding the apse, in the center the Lamb and the seven candelabra, with two symbols of the Evangelists at each side. Left and right below, all the twenty-four Elders, as they must also have appeared in the church of Ss. Cosma e Damiano before its reconstruction (p. 58).

In the apse, Christ in the center, blessing; under him, the river Jordan; above him, the Hand of God with wreath. Left of Christ, St. Paul with St. Praxedes, and far left, Paschal with square nimbus, offering a model of the church; right, St. Peter with St. Pudentiana and St. Zeno. Below, the Lamb with six lambs to either side, representing the Disciples of Christ; at the sides, the cities of Bethlehem and Jerusalem.

The Chapel of S. Zenone, built by Pope Paschal as a mausoleum for his mother Theodora, has the specifically Greek structure of the dome on the square, using squinches to modulate from the square to the circle. Since it also has a full mosaic decoration, it is one of the most remarkable Byzantine monuments of Rome.

Above the entrance is a lunette with a double circle of medallions:

INNER CIRCLE: Madonna with Christ child, Sts. Novatius and Timothy, Sts. Praxedes and Pudentiana, and other saintly women.

OUTER CIRCLE: Christ and apostles.

IN CORNERS: Four saints (the two lower of which were remade in the 13th century).

Inside the chapel:

IN THE VAULT: Christ; in the squinches, angels carrying him to Heaven.

IN THE UPPER LUNETTE (RIGHT WALL): John the Evangelist, Andrew, and James.

IN THE LOWER LUNETTE: Christ between Sts. Paschal and Valentine.

IN A SMALL NICHE OF THE ALTAR: Madonna enthroned with Christ child and Sts. Praxedes and Pudentiana.

AT THE SIDES OF A SMALL SQUARE WINDOW ABOVE THE ALTAR: St. John the Baptist, the Madonna.

IN THE LUNETTE OF THE LEFT WALL, *from left to right:* St. Agnes, Sts. Praxedes and Pudentiana.

IN THE LUNETTE OF A NICHE BELOW: Theodora (mother of Pope Paschal) wearing the square nimbus, the Madonna, and two saints. Above these, the Lamb with two adoring deer; to the right, Christ.

ABOVE THE INSIDE OF THE ENTRANCE DOOR, OPPOSITE THE ALTAR: the empty throne flanked by St. Peter and St. Paul.

S. Maria in Domnica */Via della Navicella, on the Caelian Hill/* S. Maria in Domnica is another creation of Pope Paschal; probably built on the foundation of a 7th-century building, it was reconstructed in 1513 and again in 1820. The mosaics are of Paschal's time. The arch above the apse shows Christ in a medallion, between two angels and the Apostles, and lower down, Moses (left) and Elijah (right). In the apse, the Virgin enthroned with Christ child and surrounded by angels, with Pope Paschal kneeling at her feet.

S. Marco */Via S. Marco, southwest corner of Piazza Venezia/* The church was originally built by Pope Mark in 336 and, after a restoration in 792, was reconstructed in 833 by Pope Gregory IV (828–44). The mosaics of the arch and the apse are also of the latter's time. As we see them now, the church and its mosaics are therefore a little later than the three churches that were built and decorated by Pope Paschal. The mosaics follow the pattern of Ss. Cosma e Damiano and show the same Eastern influence as Paschal's churches.

> ABOVE THE ARCH OF THE APSE: Five medallions, Christ in the center and symbols of the Evangelists on either side; below these, *left,* St. Paul, *right,* St. Peter.
>
> IN THE APSE: *center,* Christ blessing;
>> *on the right,* first Pope Mark (builder of the original church), then S. Agapitus, and far right, St. Agnes;
>> *on the left,* first St. Felicissimus, then St. Mark Evangelist, and then Pope Gregory, with square nimbus, offering the model of the church;
>> *underneath,* the Lamb, representing Christ, and twelve sheep, representing the Apostles.

S. Marco: apse mosaic

S. Clemente /*Corner of Via S. Giovanni in Laterano and Via dei Querceti*/ The church of S. Clemente consists of three layers. The lowest was originally a house with a Mithraic temple; the middle layer, a church built around 385 and dedicated to Pope Clement (d. 97), was destroyed by the Normans in 1084. The upper church, still in use today, was constructed by Pope Paschal II (1099–1118) on the ruins of the lower church.

For our purpose the lower church is of chief interest. One should not neglect, however, to look at the schola cantorum in the center nave of the upper church, because it gives an idea of the location of a similar structure, of which now only a few fragments remain, in the church of S. Maria Antiqua (p. 55). Furthermore there is to be noted an excellent example of Romanesque art in the beautiful apse mosaic of the Triumph of the Cross, mostly decorative, but also depicting lively human and animal scenes.

The lower church is especially related to the famous Slavonic missionaries of the Eastern Church, Cyril and Methodius. According to legend, they brought over to Rome from the Black Sea in the second part of the 9th century the remains of the martyred Pope Clement, which were buried here in the church named after him. Cyril died in Rome in 869 and was also buried in S. Clemente, an event commemorated by a modern mosaic in this same church.

On the walls of this lower church there are various frescoes. Some of those marked as being of the 8th and 9th centuries have Byzantine aspects, namely: Christ between the archangels Michael and Gabriel with Sts. Clement and Andrew; Ascension of Christ; Crucifixion; Descent into Limbo in the traditional Greek version; Madonna, looking like a Byzantine empress, with Child.

S. Paolo fuori le Mura /*On the Via Ostiense south of the city*/ On the spot where the Basilica of S. Paolo fuori le Mura now stands, Constantine built a basilica in honor of the great apostle. The old basilica was enlarged by his successors and, after destruction by fire, restored by Pope Leo I (440–61). It was a beautiful church adorned with mosaics, marble, etc. Unfortunately another fire struck it in 1823 and it was then rebuilt in its present state. Though much of its old splendor fell victim to the fire and the reconstruction, the new basilica retains two monuments of interest to the Byzantine traveller. They are the apse mosaic ordered by Honorius III (1215–27) and the bronze doors which, although damaged by fire, are now exhibited in the sacristy.

The mosaic, despite its late date, shows Greek elements. As we have seen (p. 44), Pope Honorius asked the Doge of Venice around 1220 (at a time, therefore, when Constantinople was held by the Crusaders of the Fourth Crusade) to send him Venetian artists for the purpose of setting up this mosaic, and these artisans were still brought up in the Greek tradition. We see Christ blessing *alla greca,* at his feet the very small figure of Honorius; right, Sts. Peter and Andrew, and left, Sts. Paul and Luke; under Christ, the altar between two angels with ten Apostles, Sts. Barnabas and Mark.

The bronze doors were given by a member of the famous Pantaleone family of Amalfi and made in Constantinople in 1070 at the order of the monk Hildebrand, archdeacon of the church, who later became Pope Gregory VII (1073–85). The doors have 54 compartments adorned by figures and ornaments, crosses, inscriptions, images of saints and prophets, evangelical scenes, from the Nativity to the Descent into Hell, and episodes of the life and martyrdom of the Apostles. A plan of the doors, describing the various subjects, is shown in the sacristy.

Ss. Quattro Coronati /*On a little square on the Via Ss. Quattro Coronati, not far from S. Clemente*/ The same indirect Greek influence through the work of Venetian artists as in S. Paolo fuori le Mura appears in the frescoes, painted in 1246, in the Oratorio di S. Silvestro of the church of the Ss. Quattro Coronati. Above, one sees the Deesis, that favorite Greek presentation of Christ between the Virgin and John the Baptist. Around the walls, a series of episodes from the life of Constantine the Great:

> Constantine, smitten by leprosy, comforts the women.
> Constantine's vision of St. Peter and St. Paul; his dispatching of messengers to Pope Sylvester (314–35), who lives isolated on a mountain.
> The Pope orders Constantine to venerate the images of the Apostles.
> The Pope heals the Emperor of his leprosy by baptism.
> Constantine conducts the Pope in splendor from his isolation back to Rome.

Evidently the frescoes convey an argument for the supremacy of the Pope in spiritual matters, putting Constantine in his place as temporal ruler.

VARIOUS

S. Maria Nova or S. Francesca Romana /Outside the Forum Romanum, north of the Arch of Titus/

Under a 12th-century picture of the Madonna in S. Maria Nova, there has recently been discovered a very old encaustic portrait of the Virgin. It is dated by some scholars as 6th/7th century, by others as 5th century. Its stern and simple structure induces some to relate it to a classic background. Encaustic icons (i.e. painted in hot wax) are very rare. Most of them are to be found in the monastery of Mount Sinai, or have been traced back to the famous icon collection there. The hot-wax technique is derived from that used in the Egyptian portraits of the deceased painted on the textile wrappers of mummies and indicates in such icons a relationship to the East.

S. Pietro in Vincoli /Piazza di S. Pietro in Vincoli near Via Cavour/

This church, much visited for Michelangelo's *Moses*, contains a 7th-century mosaic of St. Sebastian, to be found on an altar in the left aisle. It was placed there as a thank offering to the saint for having rid Rome of a pestilence in 680. Sebastian is shown in Byzantine fashion as a soldier saint; according to tradition he was an officer in Diocletian's Praetorian Guard. The date of the mosaic is probably not far from the date of the pestilence.

In the crypt is an early Christian sarcophagus containing relics of the seven Maccabee brothers, which also shows sculptures of New Testament scenes.

Triclinium Leonianum of the Lateran /Piazza di Porta S. Giovanni/

At the north side of the piazza stands a wall supporting an apse mosaic originally set up by Pope Leo III (795–816) and reconstructed nearly a thousand years later by Pope Benedict XIV (1740–58).

In its present form the mosaic does not offer much of artistic value. Its importance lies elsewhere, for it is really "an argument in mosaic" on important matters dividing East and West. The original mosaic was set up to celebrate the foundation of the Western Roman Empire when Charlemagne was crowned Roman Emperor on Christmas Day in the year 800. It also stresses the separation of spiritual and worldly powers, implying opposition to the ambition of the Byzantine emperors to be not only secular heads of the Empire but also heads of the church. It is remarkable that even at the end of the 18th century, more than three hundred years after the disappearance of Byzantium, these points were considered of enough importance to lead to the reconstruction of this argument in mosaic.

The left side of the structure shows Christ handing a key to Pope Sylvester (314–35) and a standard to the Emperor Constantine (with square nimbus), while the right side presents St. Peter honoring both Pope Leo III and the new Roman emperor Charlemagne (both with square nimbus). In the conch: Christ, center, with the four rivers of Paradise flowing from beneath his feet; left, St. Peter with four other apostles, and right, six apostles.

The Vatican Museums

• *Museo Sacro.* The part of the Vatican Museums known as the Museo Sacro contains an unparalleled treasure of small objects made of precious metals, ivory, and enamel. They range in time from the Paleo-Christian period with its hidden symbols up to, as far as Byzantine interest is concerned, the 12th century. Of this last period the small portable Byzantine mosaic of St. Theodore should be especially mentioned, as well as a stone carving of the same saint, with Greek lettering, from Southern Italy.

Secondly, there is a rich collection of early glass plaques (3rd/4th century), mostly from the catacombs. In many of these we recognize the sacred subjects frequently found in those underground chambers, such as Abraham about to sacrifice his son and the resurrection of Lazarus. A great number of the plaques are dedicated to St. Paul and St. Peter. While in these portraits the features of St. Paul, with his dark beard and the little topknot on his bald head that we know so well from later mosaics and icons, are already quite fixed, those of St. Peter are less similar to later pictures.

• *Library of the Vatican (Biblioteca Vaticana).* Entering the big hall of the Salone Sistino (No. 7), that part of the Vatican Library open to visitors of the Museum, where some of the most famous documents are exhibited, we turn to the row of tables on the left. The labels identifying the documents also give the century in which they are supposed to have been produced, but it should be kept in mind that in some cases the dating is still a matter of controversy among scholars. Of special interest are the documents numbered as follows:

1. Greek Bible, Codex B Vaticano (4th century)
2. Gospel of St. Matthew (6th century)
3. Joshua Roll (7th/8th century, considered by many to be from the 10th century); the illustrations show, *from left to right:* Joshua with prisoner kings, a battle, Joshua receives messengers
4. Cicero's *De Republica* (4th century)
5–6. Virgil's *Aeneid,* Codex Vaticano, illustrated (4th century)
7. Virgil, Codex Romano (6th century)
8. Virgil, Codex Palatino (4th/5th century)
9. Virgil's *Georgics,* Codex Augusteo (4th century)
15. Cosmas Indicopleustes, *Christian Topography* (9th century)
21. Exultet Roll from Monte Cassino, illustrated, showing Mary Magdalen and Christ (11th century)
22. Another part of the same roll, showing ornamentation
23. Exultet Roll from S. Vincenzo al Volturno (see p. 79), showing a monk or abbot offering the roll to St. Peter (10th century)

Illuminated documents of this kind are of great help to the scholar in dating other works of art, such as frescoes, since their illustrations, though in several cases copies of older pictures, betray the style of the time in which the copies were made.

GROTTAFERRATA

THE BASILIAN MONKS fleeing before the Arab conquerors of Sicily did not always find in Southern Italy the safety they had hoped for and often trekked north to escape the Saracen raids. One of these was St. Nilus of Rossano, who had founded, in 955, the monastery of S. Demetrio Corone (p. 99). When this was destroyed by the Saracens, St. Nilus fled north and, at Grottaferrata, not long before his death, a vision instructed him to found a monastery there. This he actually did, in 1004, with St. Bartholomew, also of Rossano.

The monastery and its church of S. Maria followed the Greek rites but nevertheless recognized the pope and received his protection. Thus it belongs in the category of the Uniate Eastern churches. Its Byzantine rites were looked upon with favor by the popes; although in the course of time they changed in this Latin environment, they were finally reestablished by Pope Leo XIII (1878–1903). The Credo as sung today in the service of Grottaferrata does not include the "filioque," the old point of dissension between East and West (p. 26). Altar, iconostasis, and ciborium were restored in their present form. A college for the "Italo-Greeks" was also founded by the same Pope.

Around 1475, the church and monastery, built on Roman ruins and often sacked in earlier years, were rebuilt at the orders of Cardinal Giuliano della Rovere into a fortress, a form they have retained to this day.

The church of S. Maria, consecrated in 1025 by Pope John XIX, was rebuilt in 1754 and restored in the beginning of the 20th century. In a tympanum above the entrance door to the church is a 11th/12th-century mosaic of Christ enthroned between the Virgin and John the Baptist (the Deesis; see p. 36), with a portrait of the above-mentioned St. Bartholomew.

Above the triumphal arch inside the church is a mosaic of the Pentecost, dated between the 11th and 13th centuries.

Diehl calls the mosaics of the church "toutes Byzantines," inspired by visiting Greeks. It is not certain where the artists came from, whether from among those who worked for the monastery of Monte Cassino or from elsewhere; they may even have been Venetians trained in the Byzantine style. But the fact remains that the mosaics, which also have Greek inscriptions, are Greek in concept.

The museum does not have many objects of Byzantine interest but is worth visiting if only to see the Byzantine 12th-century *omophorion* (a large episcopal stole), a very rare object indeed, worked in silk and gold with scenes of the life of Christ.

The services in the church, which has a magnificent choir, are well worth attending.

View of Stilo, with catholica in foreground

IV

BYZANTINE
ASPECTS OF
SOUTHERN ITALY

As WE HAVE SEEN, Justinian's reconquests of much of the old Roman Empire from the barbarians, at the price of neglecting his interests in the East, proved to be short-lived. The Lombards invaded Northern Italy in 568, as the Goths had done before them, and Justinian's so recent Italian successes were, at least in most of the north, soon wiped out. What remained to Byzantium, as the successor of Rome in the South, were Puglia, Calabria, and Naples. The presence of the Lombards in the South, however, proved to be a constant source of trouble to Byzantine Italy. The history of Southern Italy in this period is vague, the extent of the power and territory of the various contending governments uncertain. Eventually, there came a revival of Byzantine rule. The emperor Constantine V (741–75), in his zeal to promote his iconoclastic convictions, not shared by Rome, enhanced the importance of Southern Italy by bringing it as well as Sicily under the patriarch of Constantinople, thus withdrawing it from the power of the pope. The waning of the Lombard power then helped Byzantium to consolidate its hold on the South; for the Lombard King of Benevento, in his troubles with the German Emperor Ludwig II, placed himself under Byzantine protection in 873 and three years later ceded Bari to the Byzantines.

Though the iconoclastic controversy was now over (p. 23), the Byzantine element in Southern Italy continued to be reinforced by Greeks; these came especially from Sicily, which the Arabs had been invading since 831, their constant advances causing Greek monks and hermits to flee to Southern Italy, where they settled in caves to carry on their monastic lives. Charles Diehl (*Manuel d'art byzantin*) observes that, in conquering Southern Italy, Byzantium remade that region for several centuries into a new Greater Greece. "Under the government of the emperors the whole of the South of the peninsula again became Greek-speaking, accepted Greek habits and Greek religion, and even when the Byzantine government had disappeared there, Hellenism continued under the Norman and Angevin Kings to exercise an all-powerful influence." This influence is certainly illustrated by the appearance of these hermits and religious communities in their various caves. Though their paintings are popular in style, local and rough in execution, and frequently much damaged, they are nonetheless highly interesting. The inscriptions are often Greek, and the iconography is closely related to Eastern art. Many of the frescoes can be dated by their inscriptions as 10th/12th century (though of course there are many of later date, some of which are overpaintings).

The revival of Byzantine power in the South was marred by constant difficulties. The Lombards, though now less powerful, continued to be a source of trouble. Then the Saracens used their Sicilian stronghold to make inroads into the region, occupying much of Calabria from 840 to 880. They also occupied for a while both Bari, just retaken by the Byzantines in 876, and Taranto. Troubles with the Popes and with the German emperors kept undermining Byzantine power, and finally the Normans, those "terribili uomini del Nord," in 1071 ended Byzantine domination of Southern Italy forever. After that, the Orthodox Church, though continuing at first, began to wane and gradually almost disappeared. Yet it continues even today in the form of a so-called Uniate Church (recognizing the pope) in the Piana degli Albanesi in Sicily, and at Grottaferrata, as we have seen. Little by little, the Basilian monasteries were taken over by the Benedictines, a process so fluid and gradual that the term Basilian is not always to be understood in its original strict sense. Of their frescoes many remained, though often much damaged and overpainted; still, they are interesting enough for those who care for the art and are willing to take the trouble of finding it in places often remote and difficult of access. The visitor will be rewarded also by the beautiful landscapes in which many of these caves are located. After the Normans too had gone, the South gradually became a neglected country and a problem child of Italy.

This is the part of Italy to which refers the saying (used as the title of Carlo Levi's novel) that "Christ stopped at Eboli." It is now the working area of the Cassa per il Mezzogiorno, an organization created in 1950, five years after Levi's book was written. The Cassa has now been in full operation for over twelve years, and one is aware of its accomplishment wherever one goes, recognizing the impact it has made on the South in such a short time. Everywhere one sees the special type of concrete aqueducts for irrigation; roads and railroads are being built to form part of what economists call the infrastructure of a country; the financing of the new industries the traveler observes also comes under the purview of the Cassa. In many places signs tell that such and such monuments are being or have been restored by the Cassa. One hopes that such support in preserving the artistic treasures of the South will counteract the unfortunate fact that the sprawling infrastructure so much promoted by the Cassa does not spare the romantic aspect of the landscape. The visitor soon realizes that modern life no longer requires people to live in these delightful mountain towns for safety's sake, and that the burden of their journeys up and down the mountain may be unnecessary and uneconomical. One now frequently sees two towns bearing the same name, one situated on its original mountain site and the other in the valley below, on the railroad or on the new big highway with its huge trucks thundering by day and night. The destruction caused by the war and still quite in evidence has, of course, sped up this process of settlement in the valley.

So the South has many interesting aspects that one can take in "en passant," but our purpose was to visit, as we have done in many other countries, former Byzantine territory, and to explore what remains from Byzantine times. There are cave paintings in which Byzantine and Benedictine art are so often intermingled (in the crypt of S. Lorenzo near Fasano, for example, one sees both St. Basil and St. Benedict); there are the direct remnants of Byzantine art, as in Stilo and Rossano; and at the end there is the encounter with the monuments of the Normans and those of the Hohenstaufens (not described in this book). These last make us realize that, though Byzantine influence was not totally absent in their day, the Normans coming from the North freshly brought Western styles and habits with them and therefore did not become Easternized as they did in Sicily (see p. 119).

Itinerary of Trip in Southern Italy. Because the Byzantine monuments of Southern Italy are scattered and often hard to find, it may be helpful to outline the itinerary of our trip in that region. The Byzantine part of this trip lasted three weeks and was made in the month of April, which proved an excellent choice as far as climate was concerned. In organizing it, we found it practical to travel south from Rome along the west coast of Italy, cross the peninsula to Catanzaro, then travel south along the "toe's" east coast, come up again by the coast road all the way to Taranto, then down into the "heel," and up the Adriatic side to the "spur" (Gargano).

We had to limit our itinerary to seeing the most important Byzantine monuments. It was also necessary, of course, to group the places to be visited, in order to avoid as far as possible retracing our steps, even at the cost of missing some places otherwise worth seeing. We also tried to limit to a reasonable number the places (italicized in the itinerary) where we would stay overnight. Our twenty-three days went thus:

1—Rome to *Isernia,* via Monte Cassino.
2—From Isernia to Castel S. Vincenzo to see the Crypt of San Lorenzo; on to *Naples.*

3–6—In *Naples,* used as follows:
  3) To Capua, S. Angelo in Formis, S. Prisco.
  4) Seeing Naples.
  5) To Cimitile and Aversa.
  6) To Sessa Aurunca, Ventaroli (near Carinola), and Calvi Risorta (for the Grotta delle Formelle and Grotta dei Santi).
  7—To *Salerno,* via Amalfi, Atrani, Ravello, and Minuto.
  8—Seeing Salerno; on to *Maratea.*
9–10—In *Maratea* for a rest.
  11—From Maratea to *Catanzaro.*
  12—To Stilo, visiting Roccelletta on the way back to *Catanzaro.*
  13—From Catanzaro to *Corigliano-Calabro Stazione,* via S. Severina.
  14—To Rossano, S. Maria del Patire, and S. Demetrio Corone; back to *Corigliano.*
  15—From Corigliano to *Taranto,* via S. Maria d'Anglona.
16–19—In *Taranto,* used as follows:
  16) Matera.
  17) Fasano (for the crypt of S. Lorenzo).
  18) Massafra, Mottola.
  19) Manduria, Oria, and Veglie.
  20—Seeing Taranto; on to *Lecce,* via Brindisi.
  21—Otranto, Carpignano-Salentino, Poggiardo and Vaste just south of it (Cripta dei Ss. Stefani), Casarano (Chiesa di Casaranello, also called S. Maria della Croce); back to *Lecce.*
  22—From Lecce to *Bari,* on the way seeing cave of S. Biagio (between Brindisi and S. Vito dei Normanni).
  23—To Monte S. Angelo, to see the bronze doors; back to *Bari.*

S. Lorenzo. Starting from Rome, our first aim was to find the Crypt of S. Lorenzo, which belonged to the Benedictine abbey of S. Vincenzo, founded in 703 and destroyed by the Saracens in 881. Only the crypt escaped destruction; curiously enough, it remained unknown until 1880. We stayed the night in nearby Isernia, a place much devastated by the Second World War but still picturesque and romantic. Around it the strenuous "uphill" rural activities go on as they have for centuries.

No matter how well one plans how to approach the things one wants to see, it always works out differently in reality. Looking for the Crypt of S. Lorenzo, which we knew to be near Castel S. Vincenzo, we happened to drive past the road we should have taken to the now rebuilt abbey, on the grounds of which the crypt is situated, because it was closed off by a gate marked simply "Entry Forbidden." So we thought it best to proceed to the nearby mountain town of Castel S. Vincenzo. During our trip we found that often the search for the monuments we were interested in produced pleasant by-products—in this case, seeing the old mountain town and meeting a priest who was eager to help us. So back we went and, disregarding the no-entry sign (which proved to be just opposite another old mountain town, Cerro al Volturno, with its 15th-century castle on a hill), we followed the country road to the abbey on its plateau, where we left our car. After a short walk through fields covered with wild flowers, against a backdrop of Castel S. Vincenzo and the snowcapped Abruzzi, we crossed, on a small stone bridge, a tiny stream—none other than, some 500 yards from its source, that same Volturno we were to meet again as a full river where it runs into the sea at Castel Volturno, north of Naples.

There, dug into the hill that rises behind it, its entrance covered by a small shed-like building, was the crypt. The beautiful surroundings are a worthy introduction to the beautiful frescoes. Down a couple of steps, and directly opposite the entrance one faces a procession of four graceful female martyr saints. On the wall left of these, two martyrs, and on the wall opposite, a Madonna with the Christ child. A fine archangel in the apse and a fresco of Christ

Crypt of S. Lorenzo: archangel in apse

in the vault of the nave, though the latter is much damaged, are to be noted. After passing through the center of the crypt, one finds a Crucifixion with Mary and St. Andrew and, below, the abbot Epiphanius. The frescoes can be dated between 826 and 843 because of the portrait of Epiphanius, who was abbot of the monastery during the time they were painted.

André Grabar (*Early Medieval Painting*) calls the frescoes of high quality. He is convinced by the similarity of the iconography and the dynamic character of certain figures that they are to be considered as belonging to the Roman school. That school, however, was also making use of Byzantine conceptions, so that the S. Vincenzo frescoes have their Byzantine background.

The visit to the Crypt of S. Lorenzo provided a beginning both instructive and stimulating to our trip through the Byzantine South.

Naples. A good center from which to visit the various sites we wanted to see, Naples itself has some interesting mosaics; these are to be found in the Duomo (S. Gennaro).

From the left nave of the Duomo, one enters the Cappella di S. Restituta, at the end of the right nave of which is the Baptistery of S. Giovanni in Fonte, probably built by Bishop Soter in the second half of the 5th century.

It has remarkable mosaics of that period, which are scarce in Italy, and the chapel is therefore of special interest. Apart from their decorative flowers and birds, and the use of the symbols of the Evangelists, the mosaics recount biblical stories: St. Peter rescued by Christ from the waves, the miraculous draught of fishes, the delivery of the law (*traditio legis*) with a beardless Christ, Jesus and the Samaritan woman, the wedding at Cana. All are of good quality, though sometimes damaged.

For those seeking early Christian buildings, S. Giorgio Maggiore, near the Duomo, is of great interest. Its entrance shows remains of an early Christian church built partly in tufa, partly in brick, with arches resting on Byzantine impost capitals.

Capua. Unfortunately, Capua has suffered enormously from destruction caused by the war; moreover, it proved impossible to get access to the treasury of the Duomo. However, the rest of the day offered generous compensation by visits to nearby S. Angelo in Formis and S. Prisco.

S. Angelo in Formis. A visit to S. Angelo in Formis is an important event. Though some are partly damaged or have disappeared, frescoes still cover the greater part of the church. They are thought to be from the 11th and 12th centuries, and hence about three centuries later than those in the Crypt of San Lorenzo, which we had just visited, but the same discussions about their style are going on, if on somewhat different grounds. S. Angelo has generally been known in connection with Monte Cassino. As early as 942–44, Pope Marinus II ordered the monks of Monte Cassino to take over the church, even threatening them with excommunication if they did not obey. In practice, however, S. Angelo was included in the diocese of Capua and still belonged to Ildebrando, Bishop of Capua, in 1005. Only in 1072 did Ricardo, Prince of Capua, give the church to the Benedictines, at which time, under Desiderio (abbot of Monte Cassino from 1050–87), reconstruction began that was probably terminated by 1099.

While Byzantine influence on this Benedictine enterprise is generally acknowledged, the question is: why? Some contend that Desiderio had many contacts with Constantinople, which he had visited. Grabar (*Romanesque Paintings*) remarks that it is difficult to decide about this theory and that, on the other hand, since S. Angelo in Formis is not far from the province of Basilicata (Lucania) where the Greek monks used Byzantine models, these artisans may have exercised their influence on the local painters of S. Angelo. It is of course difficult to know whether these painters ever saw original Greek paintings or whether they worked from models that had already undergone Italian modification. Grabar's conclusion is that "it is unlikely that we shall ever ascertain the immediate sources of Sant' Angelo in Formis."

The Basilica of S. Angelo in Formis seems a simple building when one approaches it. The portico has over the entrance door the beautiful Archangel Michael (second half of 11th century), above him a Madonna looking like a Byzantine empress, with two angels (early 12th century) and, in the lunettes left and right, four charming frescoes of the Egyptian desert hermits St. Paul and St. Antony.

The basilica, built on the site of a temple of Diana, still has a pavement dating from 74 B.C. The frescoes are mostly of the 11th century, the subjects from both the Old and the New Testaments. The center apse shows Christ enthroned with the Dove above him,

S. Angelo in Formis: Archangel Michael over door

Below, *healing of the man born blind (fresco on right side of nave)*

and at left the abbot Desiderio offering him the church, a form one so often meets in apse mosaics.

The west wall is covered with a Last Judgment, the organization of which is very similar to that of the great mosaic on the west wall at Torcello. Yet it is interesting to note that the slightly later Torcello mosaic has kept, stylistically, a Byzantine aspect, which the S. Angelo fresco, though iconographically having many roots in Byzantium, has already to a great extent lost.

S. Prisco. From S. Angelo in Formis to S. Prisco is only a short distance. The Cathedral of S. Prisco—a legendary saint said to have accompanied St. Peter to Rome, later becoming the first Bishop of Capua, and whom we also meet in the name of a church built by Justinian in Constantinople for St. Priscus and St. Nicholas —does not offer any special interest in our field, but it contains a highly important small chapel, the Cappella di S. Matrona, named after Matrona, Princess of Lusitania. The chapel is the only remnant of a basilica the princess ordered built as a token of thanksgiving for being healed of a sickness after having visited the tomb of St. Priscus. It is, in fact, the tomb she had built for herself beside the basilica, and it has remarkable early 6th-century mosaics. These must originally have covered the whole interior of the chapel, but what remains is beautiful enough to make a visit to this still rather unknown spot a veritable joy.

Mosaics of that period are rare enough. The ceiling of the chapel is covered with ornamental flowers and birds; they remind us of older mosaics like the 4th-century ones of S. Costanza in Rome or those of the middle 5th century in the Mausoleum of Galla Placidia in Ravenna. One lunette shows the empty throne of the Last Judgment (see Chapter II, p. 33), so often used in the Orthodox Church, with the evangelistic symbols of the bull (St. Luke) and the eagle (St. John); the other shows Christ with the two letters Alpha and Omega (Rev. 1:8) to his left and right, respectively.

St. Priscus was much venerated in Capua, where a church was dedicated to him. Unfortunately this church, which contained 5th/ 6th-century mosaics with many saints (among whom St. Priscus appeared twice), was demolished in the middle of the 18th century. It is all the more important that we have, in this little chapel of

Cathedral of S. Prisco: the empty throne of the Last Judgment
Below, Christ, *with letters Alpha and Omega*

S. Matrona in the town of S. Prisco, mosaics of the same period as those lost in the demolition of the Capua church.

Cimitile. Next day to Cimitile, east of Naples, near Nola. The Basilica dei Martiri has some remarkable things to show. It originated as a cemetery where the first bishop of Nola, the Syriac priest St. Felix, and several later martyrs were buried. The place became so famous that by the end of the 4th century no less than four small basilicas were built there. When in 394 Paolino, a rich merchant of Bordeaux, retired thither as a monk and was joined by others, the settlement became a real monastery, a whole century before St. Benedict founded the Benedictine order. Around 400 Paolino constructed the Cappella di Papa Damaso and a fifth basilica.

We were happy to find at Cimitile an intelligent and helpful guardian, who, as often happens in such cases in Italy, knew what he was talking about. Even if one considers oneself well prepared, an interested guide can do much to enlighten one on the intricate combination of the various churches, on the remnants of decorative 5th-century mosaics in S. Felice in Pineis, and above all on the interesting but badly damaged early 8th-century frescoes in the "Basilichetta" dei Ss. Martiri, together with the early Christian frescoes of the necropolis on which that church was built, depicting Adam and Eve and the story of Jonah and the whale, so common in that period among the symbols of eternal life.

Aversa. On the way back to Naples we visited Aversa, especially interesting for the Roman ambulatory of its Duomo, built between 1053 and 1090. Here appear some gay examples of the 9th/10th-century *arte barbarica,* among them a cheerful lion with long moustaches, his tail for no apparent reason hanging across a horseman who rides right under him. We were to see a lot more of such "barbaric" art in churches; it had nothing to do with religion but served as an outlet for the artist's fantasy, of which the Romanesque, Norman, Lombard, and Gothic artisans made such extensive use. The ambulatory also shows examples of budding Gothic art.

Our last trip from Naples took us up the coast through the flat lands where the water buffaloes work in the fields and the mozzarella cheeses hang in the trees like fruits.

Sessa Aurunca. One turns inland to Sessa Aurunca. The Duomo, built between 1103 and 1113, is a pleasant building to behold. The inside has an Arabo-Romanesque pulpit with the usual huge candlestick. The colorful mosaic decoration, very Eastern, gives a special charm to the interior.

Ventaroli. Then on to Ventaroli, a town standing on the site of the old Forum of Claudius. On a little country road leading out of the town is the Basilica of S. Maria in Foro Claudio. It has three naves, each with an apse, and reminds one very much of S. Angelo in Formis. The walls carry frescoes of different periods. The central apse has an interesting fresco quite similar in composition to that in S. Angelo in Formis, though the central figure is here the Madonna with the Christ child instead of Christ. The archangel in the lower part, in S. Angelo accompanied by two other angels, is here surrounded by the Apostles. This apse fresco is thought to be 12th-century and to have been painted by a local artist.

Calvi Risorta (*Grotte dei Santi e delle Formelle*). Looking for the Grotte dei Santi e delle Formelle, we found that they are rather nearer to the new Calvi Risorta than to Calvi Vecchia. Along a road that is the old Via Latina with the usual Roman burial monuments, one comes to a place where Roman sarcophagi have been stored. There, with some luck, the guardian of the caves may be found; he first takes his clients via small hill-paths through woods and fields to the Grotta dei Santi. The grotto is quite big and is covered with paintings. They are considered to be 10th- and 11th-century, Benedictine, and painted by local monks, the Crucifixion and the St. Castrense both being 10th-century.

The Grotta delle Formelle, which lies within a half-hour's walk in the opposite direction from our starting point, has frescoes of the same period as the Grotta dei Santi.

Amalfi. The peninsula of Amalfi is, quite apart from its scenic beauty, a most interesting part of Italy. Few of the tourists milling around on the square adjoining the harbor of the city of Amalfi may realize that, while they themselves are now acting as "invisible export" (though very visible import) in the Italian balance of payments, Amalfi was for three centuries an important

Byzantine-related commercial center. Just as the Etruscans had shown in their time what importance international trade can bring to a country, Amalfi, like Salerno, Gaeta, Venice, Dubrovnik, Genoa, and Pisa, became a wealthy and even powerful entity through its ingenuity, tenacity, initiative, and diplomatic skill.

Amalfi's territory had little to offer to make it rich, but its inhabitants, hardened as they were by their fights with the Goths, the Lombards, and later the Saracens—all no mean adversaries—managed to set up a republic in 839, though in a formal sense under the suzerainty of Byzantium. Amalfi kept that status until the later part of the 11th century, coming more and more under the influence of Norman power until in the end it lost its independence to the Norman Roger II in 1131. In its heyday it had become not only rich but also politically powerful, extending its territory beyond the peninsula and putting its naval forces at the disposal of its allies. It had warehouses all over the eastern part of the Mediterranean and even settlements spread all over the south of Italy. The Amalfitan code of commercial law was in that period of glory the commercial law of all the Mediterranean.

Nor did Amalfi's citizenry neglect their religious duties. They built churches in the Near East, founded religious benevolent orders, and their famous Pantaleone family specialized in donating Constantinople-made bronze church doors, which they gave not only to the Duomo of Amalfi and to the church of nearby Atrani (below), but also to the sanctuary of Monte S. Angelo in Puglia (p. 114), to Monte Cassino (now lost), and to the Basilica of S. Paolo fuori le Mura in Rome (p. 67). These gifts show Amalfi's status at that time; a door of about the same period was sent (probably by the emperor Alexius Comnenus) from Constantinople to Venice for S. Marco. The example of the Pantaleoni was also followed by others, as when a nobleman from Salerno ordered a bronze door from Constantinople for the cathedral of his town (p. 92).

The Pantaleone generosity certainly played a large role in the creation of these bronze doors, the continued existence of which is such an asset in the study of Byzantine art. These Byzantine doors were the precursors of the 12th-century Italian-made doors of Canosa di Puglia, Troia, Trani, Ravello (below), and Monreale (p.131), which remain among the proud possessions of these places.

   • *The Duomo.* Like so many monuments in Italy, the

11th-century Duomo of Amalfi has been affected through its many alterations by the attractive Arabo-Normannic style. Its great pride are its bronze doors of 1066. They consist of twenty-four bronze plaques fixed on wood; twenty of these show crosses set on a metal background, four carry figures—Christ, the Virgin, St. Peter, St. Andrew—done in silver inlay. Some of the inlays have been partly removed, others so shined by the caressing fingers of the visitors that the gleam of the silver is now quite out of proportion to the beautiful patina of the bronze.

Atrani. Turning sharply to the right on leaving the first tunnel on the highway from Amalfi, one descends to sea level, to the small town of Atrani. Secluded thus below the big road, though so near Amalfi, the little fishing village with its beach and boats takes the visitor suddenly into its own quiet atmosphere, far from the crowds. One has to find the sacristan of S. Salvatore de' Bireto—the church so named because in it the doges of the republic of Amalfi, when elected, first donned the beret of their new dignity—to open the church and show the objects of interest; as a result, one can see them quietly. The bronze doors, again donated by a Pantaleone and like the Amalfi doors also made in Constantinople, are executed in the same technique and dated 1087, hence about 20 years later than their predecessors. The basic setup is understandably the same, although there are differences. While in Amalfi the four central panels show Christ (left) and the Virgin (right) above, and St. Andrew and St. Peter below, and Atrani the upper left panel shows the Virgin, under her St. Panteleimon (that popular Greek saint), the upper right panel St. Sebastian Martyr, and, strangely enough, *under* him, Christ.

In the church there is an interesting 11th-century marble plaque showing two peacocks, the one to the right holding a hare, with a small bird on either side; and the other, holding a human head, with a chimera on either side—one of those fantastic sculptures often produced in that period.

Ravello. Situated high above the main road and famous for the beauty of its vistas, Ravello possesses in addition the very interesting Duomo of S. Panteleimon. This church also has, as mentioned above, bronze doors executed in 1179 by Barisano da

Duomo, Amalfi: detail of left side of bronze door, showing Christ (above) and St. Andrew (below)

S. Salvatore de' Bireto, Atrani: detail of left side of bronze door, showing the Virgin (above) and St. Panteleimon (below)

Duomo of S. Panteleimon, Ravello: ambo decorated with arabizzante *mosaics, depicting Jonah and the whale.*

Trani (Puglia), which differ enormously in technique from the doors in Amalfi and Atrani. While these latter, executed in Constantinople about 100 years earlier, have only four compartments with holy persons engraved in bronze (the other twenty containing crosses), the Trani doors of Ravello depict in all their compartments either saints, stories of the Passion, or masks, in molded bronze.

Inside the church are to be noted the "arabizzante" mosaics, a delight to the eye, especially the two pulpits, one carried by six lions (two female and four male), all walking in the same direction as if they wanted to carry the whole structure across the nave, and the other with charming and colorful mosaic decoration and sea monsters related to Jonah and his "big fish."

Minuto. Not far from Ravello, across the ravine, lies Minuto, a tiny village from which one has a fine view of Ravello to complete the impression of that lovely town. It has, in the crypt of the Church of St. Nicholas, remarkable late 12th/early 13th-century frescoes that clearly show a Byzantine background, among them the Pantocrator, St. Nicholas, and the life of the Virgin, all popular Byzantine subjects.

Salerno. And so, on to Salerno. There the Duomo offers the most interest for the Byzantine-oriented traveller. Built by the Norman Robert Guiscard (d. 1085), much rebuilt but now being restored in its original form, the cathedral fronts on a large square atrium surrounded by a loggia, which produces a magnificent approach to the church. The bronze doors were ordered in 1099 by two nobles of Salerno who, like the Pantaleoni, had them executed in Constantinople. Landulf, one of the donors, appears on one panel dressed as a Byzantine patrician and showing the Byzantine title of "protosebastos." As in the Amalfi doors, most of the compartments have crosses; of the others, left, one shows two drinking hippogriffs, another, Christ, St. Peter, and St. Matthew with donors, and right, one bears an inscription, another shows St. Paul, St. Simon, and Mary.

The interior has among other things two 12th-century ambos with Sicilian "arabizzante" mosaics and the usual candelabra of the same style.

The left apse has an interesting 11th-century mosaic, only partly finished and later completed in fresco, depicting the baptism of Christ. Both the treatment of the subject and the period in which the mosaic was executed make it worthy of careful study.

Maratea. We travelled on to Maratea on the Gulf of Policastro, just above the border of Calabria, to fortify ourselves in its beautiful and restful surroundings for the trip through Calabria, Lucania (also called Basilicata, its Byzantine name) and southern Puglia.

From Maratea we crossed the peninsula to Catanzaro, situated about in the middle of the "sole" of the Italian boot. For lack of time we skipped the cathedral of Gerace, which was built in 1054 in the late Byzantine period of Calabria and restored in Swabian-Normannic times. It can easily be reached, on this run, after spending the night at Reggio Calabria. This allows one also to visit, from Brancalione Marina on the east coast, the ruins of S. Maria di Tridetti, a small 11th/12th-century Normannic church that belonged to a Basilian monastery and was already in 1200 described as in a state of decay. One reaches the cathedral of Gerace from Locri on the coast road.

Catanzaro (*Stilo and Roccelletta*). We, however, went straight from Maratea to Catanzaro to see at ease the Catholica of Stilo and the ruins of S. Maria della Roccella.

Catanzaro is situated on a deep ravine. It is not far from the sea, and the road southward along the coast is very pleasant. To reach Stilo one goes down to Monasterace Marina and then inland through beautiful valleys, the country becoming wilder and wilder. It seems that beyond Stilo the mountains become wilder still. Higher up there are a number of Basilian grottoes with Byzantine frescoes; the *Guida* of the Italian Touring Club (Vol. 21, *Basilicata e Calabria*) mentions those of S. Angelo and S. Giovanni Vecchio, and says that there are many others. One would need a guide to visit them, as they are only to be reached by mountain paths. All this shows that Stilo was at the time an important center of Byzantine monks and hermits. Though it was taken by the Normans in 1071, the Greek community evidently did not suffer much.

• *Stilo*. The town of Stilo itself can be highly recommended for its views. The ruins of the S. Nicola church with its two cupolas are interesting.

Since Greek churches are mostly modest in size, the catholica (as a Byzantine parochial church was called), which lies half hidden against the mountain above the town of Stilo, is not easily seen from afar. It is a remarkable experience to come upon a typical Greek Orthodox church in Italy, one well worth a long trip. Though a Basilian settlement was founded on this site in the 7th century, the present building dates from the 10th or 11th century.

The building itself, carefully restored, is in excellent condition. Built in brick as a square with three apses and five cupolas, it contains a number of frescoes which, despite the restoration of the whole church, unfortunately remain badly damaged. As far as discernible, they show the subjects of: John the Baptist, St. John Chrysostom (in bay of right window), St. Basil (in bay of left window), St. Nicholas, Christ (in vault above windows; 15th century), Madonna with Christ child (11/12th century), and the Assumption (on back wall).

Stilo: facade of the catholica

Roccelletta: ruins of S. Maria della Roccella

• *Roccelletta.* On our way back to Catanzaro we stopped at the little town of Roccelletta, about 1.5 km. before Catanzaro Lido, to see the ruins of an immense brick church—the Roccelletta del Vescovo di Squillace, also called S. Maria della Roccella—situated among olive groves on a large farming estate. The Roccelletta consists of the remains of a very large church (perhaps never finished), the second largest church of Calabria after the cathedral of Gerace (p. 92). The origin of the Roccelletta has been placed in the 6th century as well as in the 7th/8th, but it is now generally considered to be a Normannic structure of the 11th century. It is built in the form of a Latin cross, with three apses. Though much ruined, the huge apse and high brick walls still make an imposing impression.

S. Severina. Travelling from Catanzaro to Rossano and surroundings, we went via the picturesque mountain town of S. Severina (turn left from the coast road just before Curo). Sitting on top of its steep mountain, S. Severina overlooks the whole country around it, with its ranges of hills and valleys, and must in its time have been hard to attack. The Siberene of Roman times, the town changed its name to the present form in the 10th century. Under the Byzantine emperor Leo VI (886–912), S. Severina obtained the status of a *metropole,* thereby becoming an important Byzantine religious center. It followed the Greek rite at that time. It was conquered by the Normans in 1075, and Robert Guiscard's Norman castle must have been built on the already existing foundations of the Byzantine castle. S. Severina seems to have kept its attraction for the Greek Orthodox, for around 1400 there was an immigration of Albanians belonging to that religion. Unfortunately the Greek quarter was destroyed in the earthquake of 1783. The cathedral (13th century) has a circular baptistery with a cupola resting on eight columns, some of which were taken from pre-Christian buildings.

The little church of S. Filomena, though of Normannic times (11th/12th century), has some Eastern features. Its apse rises from the lower church, S. Maria del Pozzo (St. Mary of the Well), on top of which it is built; it has two apsidioles that are built into the thickness of the wall, and it is crowned by a cupola with a high slender drum. The lower church, which functioned as a crypt of the upper, took its name from the fact that during some period of its existence it served as a cistern for storing water.

Rossano. For anyone who has never been to Rossano, the geographic situation may be somewhat puzzling, for both Rossano and nearby Corigliano are mountain towns that now have branches below in the plain. We had to choose between Rossano and Corigliano, and as Rossano Stazione had a 4th-class hotel and lower Corigliano on the highway a 3rd-class hotel, we selected the latter. It was clean; and it had the advantage of enabling us to see something of the lively and talkative local visitors to the well-frequented bar, which served us also as sitting room. One really felt in Italy there!

As Byzantine travellers, however, what counted for us was Rossano in the mountains, and the nearby Patire and S. Demetrio Corone.

Some pamphlets call Rossano "the Ravenna of Calabria." This may seem rather overdoing it, if one thinks of mosaics, which Rossano does not possess; on the other hand, the town has so much to show of old Byzantium that one falls for its charm. In any case, it is a "must"—and no wonder. From the 8th century to the 11th, Rossano was one of the most important towns of Byzantine Italy, as one may see even now by its churches, its grottoes formerly inhabited by hermits and Basilian communities, its cathedral with a fine 11th/12th-century fresco representing the Madonna with Christ child—believed to be *achiropita* (not painted by human hands)—and, in the Museo Diocesano of the nearby palace of the Archbishop, the famous *Codex Rossanensis.*

This document, known also as the *Codex Purpureus,* is generally taken to date from the end of the 6th century. It consists of 188

S. Severina: cupola of S. Filomena

Rossano: a page from the
Codex Rossanensis, *showing*
St. Mark writing his gospel

pages, all dyed purple, with text in silver. The text, in Greek, gives
a letter from Eusebius to Carpinianus, an index to the chapters of
St. Matthew, the Gospel of St. Matthew, an index to the chapters
of St. Mark, and an incomplete Gospel of St. Mark. Its pages of
miniatures are bound together preceding the text. They illustrate
parts of the New Testament, such as the judgment of Pilate, the
despair of Judas, the Good Samaritan, the healing of the man born
blind (John 9), Jesus driving the money changers from the temple,
the wise and foolish virgins.

As Grabar points out (*La Peinture byzantine*), in the illustrations of the codex the Old Testament prophets, dressed as kings
and carrying scrolls containing their prophecies, accompany the
scenes of the Gospel to remind the reader that the New Testament
is the fulfillment of the Old; the scenes painted here are no longer
scènes de genre, but demonstrations of religious truths—in other
words, the pictures provide theological argumentation.

The origin of the codex is a much-discussed question. Though
it may well have been executed in Constantinople, other places are
not excluded. Whatever the answer, these magnificent pages clearly
show what kind of art was appreciated at the imperial court in the
6th century.

Since such a precious document cannot, of course, be handled by the public, the codex is exhibited under glass with two pages of miniatures open for inspection. During our visit one of the pages shown dealt with the wise and foolish virgins, the other with the Last Supper and the washing of the feet. As an illustrated book on the purple codex (by Antonio Munoz, Rome, 1907) is at hand, the visitor has an opportunity to examine the reproductions of those pages of the actual codex that are not exhibited.

• *La Panaghia*. Behind the cathedral is the small mid-12th-century Byzantine church of La Panaghia (The Madonna All Holy), with its three apses going down to a lower street level. In the Panaghia are some remains of frescoes that must be related to three different periods, for one can still discern the three layers on which they were painted. They are much damaged but the one of St. John Chrysostom, probably painted on a second layer, is well recognizable. The paper he has in his hand shows Greek letters. Across the tiny square from the little church is a bakery, and the white-clad bakery boys who procured the keys for us and accompanied us into the church acted as our guides, interpreting, each in his own way, what the remnants of the frescoes were supposed to represent.

• *S. Marco*. At the edge of the town, overlooking a ravine in which one can discern many grottoes that must have housed hermits and monks who lived around Byzantine Rossano, stands the Byzantine church of S. Marco (11th century). It is built (in the manner of an American split-level house) against a rising rock so that the west facade (on the high side of the rock) shows only the upper part of the church itself, while the east or rear wall, which is seen from the small square, shows the back of the crypt as well as the upper part of the church built on top of it. The east side shows the three tall apses, which nearly cover its whole height. S. Marco has five cupolas and is certainly related to the Catholica of Stilo. To get all five cupolas in one photograph, one must stand on the roof terrace of a private house opposite—and here, once again, we profited from the interest and hospitality of the kind Italians. Inside the church is a Byzantine fresco of the Madonna of the same period as the church. It is unfortunately very much damaged.

Rossano: east and north walls of S. Marco

S. Maria del Patire. The church of S. Maria del Patire (St. Mary of the Father) is not in the town of Rossano but in the country nearby, on top of another high hill. The church belonged to a Basilian monastery—the main monastery of one of the four districts of Greek monasteries in Calabria—founded just after 1100. One can still see some later-date remnants of it. The place must have been an important center of *lauras* (a group form of monastic life), one might say a sort of holy mountain, like Mt. Athos. Some polychrome decorations in the church itself clearly show Arabo-Normannic influence. The entertaining animal figures of the floor mosaic are mid-12th-century, unrelated to religious subjects.

S. Adriano. Somewhat further from Rossano lies S. Demetrio Corone with its church of S. Adriano. This church once belonged to the now-vanished monastery founded by St. Nilus of

S. Maria del Patire: detail of floor mosaic

S. Adriano: floor mosaic of serpent

Rossano in 955 and soon thereafter destroyed by the Saracens. Nilus fled north where, just before his death, he had a vision bidding him found the monastery at Grottaferrata (p. 71).

The church of S. Adriano was rebuilt between 1088 and 1106 and came under the protection of the Normans. It has since suffered much from both decay and rebuilding. It has some good 13th-century Byzantine-type frescoes: a saint on the inside of one of the arches, an interesting floor mosaic—note the beautifully executed snake!—and Byzantine capitals.

S. Maria d'Anglona. On our way to Taranto, we turned inland from Policoro toward Tursi, to see S. Maria d'Anglona, the cathedral of the now long-vanished city of Anglona, a Byzantine center with its monastery. The cathedral (no longer officially a cathedral, the bishopric having been transferred to Tursi) was started in the 11th century. Most of the frescoes are of a later date than the church, with the exception of a single Byzantine one (11th/12th centuries) that has survived in the old part of the church beside a little stairway in the right nave. It shows a judge presiding over the martyrdom of a saint.

Taranto. Old Taranto lies on an island between the Gulf of Taranto and an inland sea, the Mare Piccolo. The island is connected with the mainland at two ends by bridges. North on the mainland lies the industrial section of new Taranto, which has, among other industries, a big steel factory, a monument to the industrialization of the South; to the southeast lies the residential sector, including the hotels. Taranto itself, though it has monuments of other periods, offers very little of Byzantine interest. The Duomo (S. Cataldo) has a cupola in the Byzantine manner and decorations on the columns which are of some interest; also a crypt with Byzantine-type frescoes and an interesting early Christian sarcophagus.

Matera. Our first day in the environs of Taranto took us to Matera, capital of the province of the same name and a center for Basilian caves. It is a pleasant mountain town. A walk through the old part following the Sassi ("Stones"), a winding street along the mountain, shows a vista of many caves on the other side of the valley, some of Paleolithic times. There are also a number of caves

Matera: rock church of S. Barbara

Crypt of S. Lorenzo: entrance

in parts of the old town. The monks and hermits, while loving solitude, must nevertheless have depended on the town for their living, but left as it expanded.

We had read in an Italian periodical an article on an organization of young men, deeply interested in their province of Matera, who made a thorough investigation of the grottoes around the town of Matera; in fact, the article said they had already discovered no less than 130 Basilian caves, many of which they have measured and photographed. They had formed an organization called "La Scaletta."

We got into contact with this group of young men, and they were kind enough to show us the rock church of S. Giovanni in Monte Errone, situated in the Sasso Caveoso, with many frescoes, some from 1190, some older. Further, the rock church of S. Barbara (now under a cement factory), the construction of which shows two columns, a nave, iconostasis, and bema, all excavated in the rock. The partly ruined church of S. Gregorio is interesting for its Byzantine architecture, and it has some remnants of frescoes.

To see some of the 130 caves roundabout would take not only considerable time but also the same sort of good guidance. The colony of Basilian monks must have been extensive.

Fasano (*Crypt of S. Lorenzo*). To go to the Crypt of S. Lorenzo near Fasano, one takes the road from Fasano to Savelletri. At a fork, one sticks to the right-hand road (the left goes to the railroad station) and finds on the right, before the road passes under the railroad, a shallow valley in which the crypt is situated. The valley is, however, so full of caves, any of which might be the Crypt of S. Lorenzo, that one really needs a guide. We found a farmer working in his vineyard, who offered to send his son, and with him we walked for about a mile, in and out of overgrown and wooded fields, to reach the cave, which otherwise we might easily have missed entirely.

The cave of S. Lorenzo is unfortunately much damaged but is still well worth visiting. It has an iconostasis and, in the presbytery, interesting frescoes: Christ in the image of the Deesis (with St. John and the Virgin), and nearby St. Basil and St. Benedict peacefully together. The frescoes are thought to be 12th-century.

Crypt of S. Lorenzo: Christ (in fresco of Deesis)

Massafra: valley near church of the Madonna della Scala

Massafra. From Taranto one can also see the various caves of Massafra. This town was ideally situated for the settlement of hermits because of the deep ravine dividing it in two. All crypts are easily reachable, but as there are so many it is advisable to find a guide to set one on the right course.

Under the hospital of Matteo Pagliari is the Crypt of S. Antonio Abbate, probably 10th/11th-century. The frescoes, much damaged, are of various periods (12th to 18th centuries) and of a very rural character.

The church of the Madonna della Scala is an 18th-century structure, a kilometer out of the town where broad stairs lead half-way down the valley to the spot where once there was a settlement of Greek monks. Over the main 18th-century marble altar there is a Madonna with Byzantine characteristics (probably 12th century), adored by two kneeling deer. According to a legend, deer came regularly and knelt near the place where the picture of the Madonna was found. Along the side of the rocky valley opposite the church one sees a great number of caves, indicating that many hermits must have found this a suitable place to settle in.

On the left as one leaves the church is the Cripta della Buona Nuova (Crypt of the Good Tidings), on the spot where the deer found the Madonna. In the Crypt is another Madonna (13th century) and a fresco of Christ Pantocrator.

The crypt of S. Leonardo has a great number of saints on the arches, and, in the apse, Christ enthroned in the image of the Deesis.

The crypt of S. Marco has frescoes, probably 13th/14th-century.

Opposite S. Marco, on the other side of the valley and practically at the same level, is the Crypt of the Candelora. Here we find a number of interesting frescoes: in the narthex, the Presentation in the Temple, beautiful in color (probably 13th/14th century), and in arches of the church a great many pictures of saints, and a Madonna *orans* with Christ child, some of which have unfortunately been badly damaged.

Mottola. In Mottola, there are a number of interesting caves. Two of the best known are situated on the Masseria (farm) of Casalrotto, about 3 kilometers from Mottola, where there was a Benedictine abbey. They are the the Crypt of S. Nicola and the Crypt of S. Margherita. We chose to go to the former, but the question first was how to find the Masseria, then the crypt. The only thing was to ask. It was Sunday and Mottola's big square, into which we drove and which in fact serves as a club for the population, was full of people. This square was presided over, in the literal sense of the word, by a portly and magnificent policeman, who proved to be very helpful. When we explained our problem, he said the man we needed was a certain Don Michele, a local lawyer, journalist, and—what was very important for us—a historian of the area in his own right. Fortunately Don Michele was sitting on a bench nearby and proved well pleased to guide us. A retired rural gendarme, who knew the place we wanted to see very well, joined the group and we all packed in for the drive to the Masseria Casalrotto. There the successor to our gendarme joined us, and the whole company walked, winding through olive and lemon groves in an enchanting valley all covered with wild flowers, to the rock in which the crypt is excavated.

The crypt is a chapel consisting of three naves divided by columns and arches. The frescoes are numerous and generally well preserved. They belong to two periods, sometimes a later layer painted over an older, in which case the first layer is probably 11th-century, while the second layer, which often repeats the older motive, may be as recent as the 14th or 15th centuries. An example appears on a column on which the second layer shows a St. Nicholas while the old layer under it reveals the same subject, probably the original decoration. An interesting Deesis may be dated 11th/12th century. Even if a great number of the paintings belong to a later period, the subjects betray their Byzantine origin by the appearance of such saints as Basil and Helena. Our visit to the cave was most rewarding, made more so by the experience of friendly Italian helpfulness that had made it possible.

Manduria. East of Taranto we set forth to visit Manduria, Oria, and Veglie. In Manduria one finds the Crypt of S. Pietro Mandurino (8th or 9th century). The frescoes are in good shape, but while the original paintings in the sanctuary must have been interesting, they were unfortunately totally done over at the end of the 18th century or the beginning of the 19th.

Oria. Situated on a mountain overlooking the valley, with its *castello* originally built by Frederick II, Oria is one of

Mottola: exterior of crypt of S. Nicola; with visitors (from left to right: Don Michele, Mrs. Nikolajević, the two gendarmes, and the author's wife)

Crypt of S. Nicola: two layers of frescoes of St. Nicholas

those pleasant Italian towns one should not miss. After entering the *castello* one finds, in the right-hand corner of the yard, the Crypt or Chapel of S. Maria, called also of Ss. Crisante e Daria, and thought to be 9th-century. It is probably the crypt of the old cathedral or a cistern later rebuilt into a church. The frescoes, thought to be 11th- or 12th-century, are, alas, very much spoiled. But the chapel itself, cut as it is out of the solid rock, is a very interesting structure well worth studying.

Veglie (*Cripta della Favana*). In Veglie is the Convento della Favana, a formerly Franciscan monastery, now owned by the city. Close to the entrance of the monastery is the Cripta della Favana, which has a great number of frescoes, mostly of later periods. Some may be as late as the 15th century; these have a local and somewhat rough character but provide a highly effective decoration. Some show special features, such as an unusual Trinity with God the Father in the form of the Ancient of Days (Daniel 7:9), the Holy Spirit as a dove, and Christ on the cross. While around the late 13th and early 14th centuries, though not before that period, the Trinity may occur with Father, Son, and Holy Ghost, the appearance of Christ on the cross in this connection is rare. The crypt calls for special attention; it is pitch dark, and a strong flashlight is necessary.

Brindisi. Driving from Taranto to Lecce we spent some time in Brindisi, where we were struck by two traffic signs, one pointing to the Via Appia and one to the Via Egnatia. It was in Brindisi that these two great roads linking Rome and Constantinople may be said to have met, for from Brindisi the ships crossed to Dyrrhachion (now Durazzo in Albania), where the Via Egnatia started. We spent our time in the Church of S. Maria del Casale, near the airport, about 3.4 km. from the center of Brindisi. This church was built in 1320 by Philip of Anjou. A visit is not too easy because it is normally closed; though, according to the *Guida d'Italia,* the key should be available at the local information office (E.P.T.), nobody seemed to know about it there. We were in luck, however, for when we arrived at the church a wedding was going on and after that the doors remained open. The frescoes that cover much of the walls are to a great extent 14th-century. They clearly show their Byzantine background as well as their Gothic parentage. As in Torcello, near Venice, and in S. Angelo in Formis, the west wall is totally covered by a Last Judgment, here in fresco. In the apse, Life and Ascension of Christ, and on the east wall, Christ enthroned between angels.

Carpignano Salentino. The Cripta delle Ss. Christina e Marina in Carpignano Salentino, which was our first visit next day, is entered from the Piazza Madonna delle Grazie. This crypt is among the most important in the South. It contains frescoes of various periods, among them two images of Christ enthroned, with Greek inscriptions, signed, and to be dated respectively 959 and 1020.

Two stairways descend into the crypt. Taking the right-hand one, the right wall has the most interesting frescoes: in the niche on the left, Christ (959); left of this niche, the Virgin, and right of it, the Angel of the Annunciation. It may be taken that the two latter are of the same period as the fresco of Christ. Further to the right, the Virgin with Christ child, and in the niche far right, the other Christ (1020). Diehl considers these frescoes of the greatest importance and thinks there is no Basilian painting in the south of Italy older than the elder of these two Christs, save in manuscripts.

Cripta delle Ss. Cristina e Marina:
Archangel of the Annunciation

On the wide pillar in front of the right wall is a fresco of St. Nicholas (?) flanked by St. Theodore (left) and St. Christina (right), which is 13th-century.

On the left wall St. Christina appears, probably 15th-century. The figures of St. Theodore and St. Nicholas opposite the left-hand stairs are probably also 15th-century.

Otranto. So near to Greece, Otranto was for centuries (though with some interruptions) an important Byzantine center in Southern Italy and one of the last bulwarks holding out against the Norman conquests. With Byzantium's growing influence in Southern Italy, it had, under the Emperor Leo VI (886–912), obtained archiepiscopal status, and under Nicephoras II Phocas (963–69) that of *metropole,* with authority over such faraway places as Acerenza, Tursi, Gravina, Matera, and Trirarico.

Otranto has two churches of interest, the Cathedral (Annunziata) and the little S. Pietro. The floor of the Cathedral is covered with fantastic mosaics made by a priest named Pantaleone in 1163–66, rather rough and related to *arte barbarica* yet also including some biblical stories. These mosaics have a special value of their own. One of them shows the ascension of Alexander the Great, borne upward by two griffins—the motive which in Romanesque art represented pride; one sees it also on the north facade of S. Marco in Venice.

The big crypt is worth visiting. It has a great number of columns, some of which are Byzantine. The walls bear Byzantine-type frescoes, among which should be noted a Madonna with Christ child.

S. Pietro is a 10th/11th-century Byzantine structure containing a number of frescoes of different periods. Unusual in presentation are a Baptism of Christ and, particularly, the picture of Christ expelling Adam and Eve from the Garden of Eden.

Poggiardo. The fame of the frescoes in the crypt of S. Maria in Poggiardo took us to that town. They were only discovered in 1929 and have thus remained free from damaging influences. To our great disappointment, they had been taken off the walls and brought to Rome to be restored.

Cathedral, Otranto: floor mosaic of Noah

Below, *secular floor mosaic*

Vaste (for Ss. Stefani). From Poggiardo it is about 1 km. in the direction of S. Cesarea to Vaste, and in Vaste it was not difficult to find the way to the Cripta dei Ss. Stefani, starting out appropriately from the main street along the Via dei Ss. Stefani and walking through a prosperous rural landscape. The crypt is considered among the most important of the region. It is a full-fledged small basilica with three naves divided by two rows of three pillars each. Each nave has an apse. The frescoes are of different periods, ranging from the 12th to the 15th century. They are of good quality but many are unfortunately very much spoiled.

The left apse shows a 12th-century fresco of Sts. Basil, Nicholas, and Gregory of Nianzus, all Eastern saints. In the central apse a fresco, probably two centuries later than the foregoing, depicts the Virgin *orans*, with (probably) John the Evangelist. Right of the Virgin are three figures dressed alike in blue; a similar figure appears in another fresco, that of St. Catherine, where its position could indicate that of a donor. The right apse contains the figure of Christ between the archangels Michael and Gabriel. On the pillars we see two frescoes of St. Stephen and two of St. Antony.

Casarano. Then to Casarano, to visit the Chiesa di Casaranello or S. Maria della Croce, part of which is all that is left of the old town, now disappeared. The church has several interesting mosaics of the 5th century: in the cupola, a cross with stars; in the presbytery, geometric figures as well as birds and animals, which really seem like floor mosaics raised to the ceiling. The frescoes on the walls show 13th-century stories of St. Catherine and of the New Testament.

S. Biagio. On the way to Bari next day we stopped to see the cave of S. Biagio (St. Blaise). Taking the bypass around Brindisi one branches off on the road to S. Vito dei Normanni. After crossing the railroad by the overpass one passes on the right a long row of cypresses, and at milestone 548 (at right) there is a country road that leads, after one crosses the railway tracks and keeps right at a fork, to the Masseria Iannuzzo. Bearing right again, one finds the crypt in a rocky formation on one's right.

The ceiling of the crypt is entirely painted, as are the walls. Unfortunately the wall frescoes are much damaged. According to

S. Pietro, Otranto: Baptism of Christ

S. Biagio: the Ancient of Days

some, the crypt was painted in the 11th and 12th centuries (possibly a century later) and finished by a mediocre artist in the 14th/15th century.

The main subjects on the ceiling are: the Annunciation, the Presentation in the Temple, the Flight into Egypt, the Entry into Jerusalem, and the Ancient of Days, blessing and looking very much like Christ. Around him the four Evangelists and two seraphim and, further left and right, Daniel (who holds a script referring to Daniel 7:2 and 9) and Ezekiel. Right of the Ancient of Days are written words of Daniel 7:9. As Daniel's description—"his raiment was white as snow and the hair of his head like pure wool; his throne was fiery flames"—does not tally with the picture of the Ancient of Days, it is possible that this figure in fact represents Christ, though then the quotation remains a mystery.

On the right wall we see St. Andrew and St. John the Evangelist, St. Blaise, St. Nicholas. On the back wall, St. George with Sts. Demetrius and Nicholas, the Nativity, the Epiphany, St. Sylvester, and St. Stephen.

Bari. Southern Italy under Byzantine rule went through many vicissitudes. Of these, Bari in Puglia had its share, though it always seemed to recover and even had strong comebacks as in the days of the Byzantine Emperor Leo III (717–41). After the Saracen occupation it was retaken by Byzantium in 876 and even became the capital of Byzantine Italy (p. 26).

While a great part of Southern Italy abounded with Greek monasteries and churches, of which a number still remain (Stilo, Rossano, S. Pietro in Otranto, and others), the Bari region has no large Byzantine monuments. There are crypts around Altamura, where there is also the church of S. Nicola dei Greci, which followed the Greek rite until 1601. Andria has its crypts, as well as Gravina di Puglia, Monopoli, and Putignano. In these smaller religious entities one sees the influence of Basilian monks who certainly came from the South, though comparatively few seem to have got as far as the Bari region. The bronze doors of Amalfi, Atrani, and Salerno, as we know, were still ordered in Byzantium in the 11th century, but apart from those given by a Pantaleone to the sanctuary of S. Michele in Monte S. Angelo, the bronze doors of Puglia are not Byzantine. Even the Eastern features in the doors of

Bohemund's tomb at Canosa do not derive from direct Byzantine influence, but are a reminder of Bohemund's Crusader activities.

After they had conquered Bari and Brindisi in 1071, the Normans gradually conquered Sicily, unifying it with Southern Italy in 1127. While in Sicily the Norman builders showed their appreciation for Byzantine art, on the peninsula there are few signs of this having been the case. In fact, while we go to Sicily for Byzantine-inspired art—to see in or near Palermo the Martorana, the Palatine Chapel, Cefalù, Monreale, all built from around the middle to the end of the 12th century—we find in Bari and its surroundings—in the Cathedral of S. Sabina in Bari, the Cathedral and churches of Molfetta and Trani, Barletta, Palo del Colle, Bitonto, which are all of the same period as the Sicilian ones named—hardly any Byzantine influence. And though we owe to the Hohenstaufen Frederick II, who was not averse to Eastern splendor, many buildings in Puglia, where he lived most of the time, he did not follow his Sicily-based predecessors in their preference for the Byzantine. The Normannic churches remained for the greater part unpainted, whereas the Benedictines (S. Angelo in Formis is an outstanding example), though changing the style, continued painting in a manner inspired by Byzantium. In fact, frescoes like those of the 14th century in S. Maria del Casale in Brindisi (p. 108), which show Gothic trends, are still based on Byzantine sources.

It is of course in this region that the Normans coming from the north were inspired by Romanesque art, but the change to Byzantine taste they underwent in Sicily did not spread to Southern Italy, which the Palermo-based rulers may well have considered "provincial."

Though Byzantine-oriented and accordingly confining his attention to his special field, the traveller in Southern Italy will not fail to profit from being in Bari to visit the many magnificent Norman castles and churches in which the region abounds.

Monreale: view of the cathedral

V

BYZANTINE
ASPECTS OF SICILY

BECAUSE OF ITS geographical situation Sicily was always coveted by any nation striving for power. Only a short distance from Africa and close to Italy, the great island formed an excellent springboard for strategic action between the two continents. The Greeks realized this; they came to Sicily as early as 735 B.C. So did the Carthaginians when they became rivals of the Greeks in 413 B.C. As Greek control deteriorated, the Romans were called in for assistance, which led to Sicily becoming a Roman province in 210 B.C. The Romans developed its economy to a point where it became "the granary of Italy," a condition certainly contrasting with the bareness of the country as we see it today; as the Cassa per il Mezzorgiorno is doing the same work there as its forefathers did, Sicily may perhaps in the future once again serve its former purpose!

The Christian church seemed to have made good progress in Sicily after the end of the 3rd century, but the country suffered, like the Italian mainland, from inroads by the Ostrogoths and invasions by the Vandals from Africa.

Justinian and his famous general Belisarius of course saw the importance of again adding Sicily to the Roman Empire, and this they succeeded in doing in 535. When after Justinian's death most of Italy was lost again, Sicily, like the south of Italy, still remained part of the Empire.

Like Sicily's earlier rulers, the Byzantines appreciated the island's strategic and economic position as well as its climate and scenic beauty, so much so in fact that when the Emperor Constans II (641–68) visited the island in 663, he decided to move his residence to Syracuse. However, as could have been foreseen, Constantinople was not inclined to give up its position as a capital, and after Constans was murdered in Syracuse in 668 the imperial residence remained Constantinople.

Constantine V (741–75) brought Sicily under the patriarch of Constantinople, just as he did Byzantine Southern Italy, withdrawing it from the power of the pope and stressing the importance of Sicily to Byzantium. It was the Saracens who brought about the fall of Byzantine Sicily. Starting in 827, they gradually conquered the whole island, with a small exception in its eastern part, which was also lost in 902, though later regained for a few years (1038–43). The Saracens used the geographical advantages of Sicily also for making frequent inroads into Southern Italy, causing great damage there and increasing the political instability.

Sicily never returned to the Byzantine fold. The Normans gradually ousted the Saracens after Robert de Hauteville (surnamed Guiscard, the shrewd one) in 1061 ordered his brother Roger to invade the island from Southern Italy.

From the Greek period we still admire several extensive ruins, the tremendous floor mosaics of the Piazza Armerina remind us of the Roman times, the Arabs have bequeathed us the partly Eastern character of Sicily, and the Normans their architecture. Except for some Basilian grottoes in the east, it is true that no Byzantine monuments remain from the time of the Byzantine government in Sicily, but because the Normans and their immediate successors acquired from the Eastern atmosphere a taste for Byzantine splendor, we go to Sicily for some of the finest examples of Byzantine mosaics—which, however, were created in Norman times.

The succession of the Norman rulers of Sicily was as follows (the first and last of them left no major monuments):

Roger I de Hauteville (1061–1101)
Roger II (1112–54, after a regency by his mother), who became
      Sicily's first king in 1130
William I (1154–66)
William II (1171–89, also after a regency by his mother)
Tancred, a Hauteville bastard (1189–94)

After a short regency by Tancred's widow, the house of Hohenstaufen unseated the house of de Hauteville when the Roman Emperor, Henry VI of Hohenstaufen (1194–98), who was married to Roger II's daughter Costanza, successfully claimed the throne.

His son, the colorful Frederick II, reigned from 1212 to 1250, after an intervening regency by his mother Costanza. Frederick II was crowned Roman Emperor in 1220. He lived most of his life outside of Sicily, yet was buried in a porphyry sarcophagus in Palermo.

If there is any region showing that Byzantine art is not necessarily tied to Byzantine power, it is Sicily. The great mosaic church decorations are Byzantine, though set up in a period when the rulers were Normans, their religion Roman Catholic. Neither the Byzantine emperor nor the Orthodox patriarchs now had any say there. It even came to war between Sicily and Byzantium when the Byzantine emperor John II Comnenus (1118–43), worried by the crowning in 1130 of Roger II as king over Sicily and by the special position of the Normans in the Crusades, allied himself with Germany and Pisa against Sicily. In 1156 the Norman king William I defeated the Byzantines at Brindisi, and peace was finally made in 1158.

After this peace the Normans again attacked Byzantium, conquering territory between Dyrrhachion (Durazzo in Albania) and Thessalonica, and losing it again. After the death (1198) of King William II, the Roman and German Emperor Henry VI, a Hohenstaufen, became also King of Sicily, and, identified as he was with a Germany inimical to Byzantium, reclaimed the lost territory, asking an annual tribute so huge that Byzantium could only pay it by despoiling the imperial tombs of the Church of the Holy Apostles in Constantinople.

Yet it was under Norman rulers that these great monuments of Sicily, all with Byzantine decorations, were built:

Under Roger II: the Cathedral of Cefalù, the Palatine Chapel, and the Church of the Martorana;

Under William I: the room in the Norman Palace in Palermo, the so-called Stanza di Ruggiero;

Under William II: the palace of Zisa, and the great Cathedral of Monreale.

The custom, also, that began with Roger II's burial in a porphyry tomb—porphyry being especially related to Byzantine imperial dignity as well as being used by the popes for their tombs—continued in the cases of William I, Henry VI, and Frederick II; this last example shows that, at a time when Constantinople was in the hands of the Crusaders, its enemies in Sicily still honored Byzantine glory by the use of its symbols of majesty (see below, p. 139).

In the light of the tensions and hostilities between Sicily and Byzantium, the question naturally arises: who were the artists who produced the mosaics and where did they come from? Professor Demus (*The Mosaics of Norman Sicily*) points out that they must have come to a large extent from Byzantium and quotes examples of periods of rapprochement during which this would actually have been possible. Such could well have been the case in Roger's time in the hiring of Greek workers to set up the mosaics for the Palatina, the Martorana, and Cefalù, while William II's contacts with Byzantium may have brought him the opportunity of engaging mosaicists for Monreale. Surely such Greek artists must have trained Sicilian pupils.

MONUMENTS FROM THE TIME
OF ROGER II

Cefalù. A short drive eastward from Palermo brings the visitor to Cefalù. Its church, against the background of an imposing rock, forms a magnificent spectacle.

The building, on the whole Western in character, combines, according to Demus, Northern and Southern Italian elements as well as typically Sicilian features. The Norman character of the big towers flanking the facade has parallels in Southern Italy.

The eastern part of the building and the apse mosaics were finished in 1148, but the remainder of the building was only completed under William I, as his father Roger II, who had started it, at a certain point lost interest for ecclesiastical reasons. This explains why the cathedral does not have the full mosaic decorations one finds in the Palermo churches and in Monreale, although William I, apart from completing the building, also added other mosaics in the second half of the 12th century.

The church is a basilica without a cupola, and therefore, on entering its great space, one finds the holy persons in the hierarchy in other locations than those customary in a Greek cupola church—where, for instance, the Pantocrator is in the dome. Here Christ has come into the conch of the apse, a dark-haired Christ whose raised right hand very clearly demonstrates the gesture of blessing *alla*

Cefalù: the Pantocrator

greca. Under him, the Virgin *orans,* flanked by four archangels who carry symbols of the Eucharist. Underneath, left and right of a dividing window, in two rows, the Apostles:

UPPER TIER, *from center outward:*
> *left,* Peter with cross, staff, scroll, and keys, Matthew, Mark;
> *right,* Paul, John, Luke.

LOWER TIER:
> *left,* Andrew with cross-topped staff, James, Philip;
> *right,* Simon, Bartholomew, Thomas;
> *at the bottom,* inscription dated 1148.

Vault and side-walls of the presbytery are covered by mosaics, of a somewhat later date (Demus puts it at 1150–60). The four compartments of the vault each contain a six-winged angel, marked Seraphim in north and south, Cherubim in west and east, the latter two also having an angel in each side angle.

The left and right walls of the presbytery are fully covered with mosaics set in four rows:

South (right) Wall

FIRST *(top)* ROW: Abraham (half-figure in medallion), between David and Solomon.

SECOND ROW: Three prophets, Jonah left of window, Micah and Nahum, right.

THIRD ROW: Four warrior saints venerated in the Greek Church, but with their names written in Latin: Theodore, George, Demetrius, Nestor.

FOURTH *(bottom)* ROW: Four Greek saints, their names written in Greek: left of window, Nicholas, and right, Basil, John Chrysostom, Gregory the Theologian.

North (left) Wall

FIRST *(top)* ROW: Melchisedec (half-figure in medallion), between Hosea and Moses.

SECOND ROW: Three prophets, Joel and Amos left of window, Obadiah, right.

THIRD ROW: Holy deacons, Sts. Vincent and Lawrence left of window, with Peter of Alexandria; St. Stephen, right.

FOURTH *(bottom)* ROW: Sts. Gregory, Augustine, Sylvester, left of window, Dionysius the Areopagite, right, all named in Latin.

The Palatine Chapel. Consecrated in 1140, the Palatine Chapel forms part of the Norman Palace. Its architecture "follows

[ON OPPOSITE PAGE] *Cefalù: mosaic in lower right of apse*

the mature type of Norman ecclesiastical architecture of Sicily. Cefalù, founded just a year before the Palatine chapel, had been a tentative combination of Northern and South-Italian elements. In the Palatina there are no Northern traits. . . . The ground plan is a synthesis of Greek and Italian forms, in fact" (Demus). The East was making itself felt. The inscriptions, however, are Greek in the older mosaics and Latin in the later.

The interior of the building is almost completely covered with mosaics. Though most of these date from Roger II, some, such as those in the aisles, are of the time of his successor William I; in addition, later alterations have changed the aspect of many of the decorations. Part of the mosaics of the north wall were destroyed in 1798.

The chapel has a cupola, hence the Pantocrator is in the usual place. But, following the pattern of Cefalù, there is also a Pantocrator in the conch of the apse and, below him, the Virgin (18th-century), the four standing figures flanking her being, left, Mary Magdalen and Peter, right, John the Baptist and James.

The central square under the cupola is supported by four arches:

EAST ARCH: Annunciation.
WEST ARCH: Presentation in the Temple (both these subjects flow over into the north and south walls).
SOUTH ARCH: Mary's throne and the city of Nazareth; three medallions of Prophets (Hosea, Zephaniah, Malachi); Joseph (part of the Presentation in the Temple).
NORTH ARCH: at the right, Gabriel's foot (from the Annunciation); medallions of Amos, Obadiah, and Habakkuk; further left, parts of the Presentation.

In the angular squinches above are the four Evangelists, seated. In the four flat niches between the squinches, the four Prophets, David, John the Baptist, Solomon, and Zachariah, and in the eight places between the flat niches and the squinches, eight more prophets: Isaiah, Ezekiel, Jeremiah, Jonah, Daniel, Moses, Elijah, and Elisha. Between the windows in the dome, around the Pantocrator, are, in the western half, the four archangels, grandly Byzantine-clad; in the eastern half, four angels.

In the south transept, in the conch of the east wall, St. Paul, with the Nativity above. In the vault, Pentecost.

The south wall of the south transept continues the Gospel story

Palatine Chapel: Esau hunting birds, on north wall of nave

*Palatine Chapel: Nazareth,
on south arch
of central square*

(begun with the Annunciation on the east arch), showing Joseph's dream, the flight into Egypt, the baptism of Christ, the Transfiguration, the raising of Lazarus, and the entry into Jerusalem.

The north transept has suffered much. In the conch of its east wall, St. Andrew; below, Sts. Joseph, Barnabas, Stephen. Above the conch, Virgin and Child (in attitude of *hodegetria,* showing the way). In vault, the Ascension.

The nave, with its picturesque colors and its narratives, is full of life. It is mainly devoted to mosaics of the Old Testament, in two tiers above the arches:

Upper Row

SOUTH WALL, *starting from the east end:* scenes from the creation of the universe—division of the waters; creation of dry land and plants; creation of sun, moon, and stars; creation of fishes and birds; creation of quadrupeds and man; Adam introduced into Paradise; the creation of Eve.

NORTH WALL, *starting from the west end:* the Original Sin; judgment of Adam and Eve; expulsion from Paradise; Adam and Eve working; the story of Cain and Abel; lastly (following three mosaics of later date), the building of Noah's ark.

Lower Row

SOUTH WALL, *starting from the east end:* Noah in the ark and Noah's drunkenness; the building of the Tower of Babel; Abraham's hospitality to the angels; the hospitality of Lot.

NORTH WALL, *starting from the west end:* the destruction of Sodom; the sacrifice of Isaac; Rebecca at the well; the life of Jacob; the blessing of Isaac (to be noted is the representation of Esau hunting birds, one of the rare secular scenes in Byzantine mosaics); Jacob's dream; Jacob wrestling with the angel.

The walls further show many pictures of saints.

The Martorana. In the center of Palermo stands the Church of the Martorana, the mosaics of which have been called the most Byzantine in Sicily. Much altered as we see it today, it was founded as an Orthodox church in 1143 by George of Antioch, admiral of the fleet of Roger II, who wanted to remain faithful to his religion. All the mosaics are considered to date between 1143 and 1151. Their texts are Greek and the iconography shows Byzantine prototypes.

Martorana: mosaics in narthex, showing, left, George of Antioch offering the church to the Virgin and, right, Roger II being crowned by Christ

Entering the narthex, we see two interesting mosaics: left, the Madonna with the tiny figure of the admiral humbly prostrated at her feet, and right, Roger II being crowned by Christ.

In the cupola, the Pantocrator enthroned, surrounded by the four archangels with veiled hands. In the drum, eight prophets: Jeremiah, Isaiah, David, Moses, Zachariah, Daniel, Elisha, Elijah. In the squinches below are the four Evangelists.

As in the Palatine chapel, the Annunciation appears over the east arch of the central square and the Presentation in the Temple over the opposite (west) arch.

In the barrel-vaults of the transept, south and north, are eight of the Apostles.

The vault of the bema shows the archangels Michael and Gabriel.

The main apse was destroyed but, according to Demus, must have contained the Virgin, flanked by the still existing images of Joachim and Anna in the conches of the side apses.

In the vault to the west of the central square are the Nativity of Christ and the Death of the Virgin.

On the south wall of the transept are three saints, Cyrus, John, and (a half-figure in a medallion above the window) Hermolaos.

MONUMENTS FROM THE TIME OF WILLIAM I

Norman Stanza (*Stanza di Ruggiero*). The name of this room in the Norman Palace is misleading, since it suggests that the mosaics date from Roger II's time; in fact, they are probably from the last years of William I or even a little later, during the regency preceding the reign of William II (i.e. between 1160 and 1170).

Mosaics of secular subjects like these of the Stanza are all the more welcome since, once very popular, they are now extremely rare, so many of the secular buildings they adorned being no longer extant. Apart from pure decorative and plant motives, the big room in the palace shows a great and entertaining variety of beautifully executed animal figures: peacocks, lions, eagles, deer (with hunters), swans, leopards, etc.

Martorana: the cupola

*Martorana: Virgin of the
Annunciation, on south side
of east arch*

Norman Stanza: *mosaic with centaurs and animals*

Below, *mosaic with animals and hunters*

MONUMENTS FROM THE TIME
OF WILLIAM II

Palace of Zisa. This palace, just outside of Palermo, was started under William I and finished under William II. A few of its secular mosaics (set up probably in the beginning of the reign of William II) remain; they are in certain respects similar to some of the mosaics in the Palatine Chapel and in Monreale.

Monreale
. . . The mosaics of Monreale will have to be regarded as the outstanding monument of the last phase of middle Byzantine church decoration, as a monument which shows that Byzantine Art was not on the decline towards the end of the twelfth century, but vigorous enough to produce a novel mode of composition, a new way of rendering an event and a new style. (Demus, *The Mosaics of Norman Sicily,* preface, p. xix.)

Roger II possessed a castle in a park that included the place where the Cathedral of Monreale and its adjoining cloister now stand. His grandson William II (the Good) dedicated part of this property to his new foundation, the cathedral and monastery built to replace a small chapel that during the Saracen occupation had been the see of the Greek Metropolitan of Palermo. The pope gave the monastery, which was to follow Benedictine rule, a great independence and also granted special powers to the king. The first charter was issued by William II on August 15, 1176, endowing the monastery with many possessions in Sicily, Calabria, and Puglia, including S. Marco in Rossano (Calabria) and the whole city of Bitetto near Bari in Puglia. On February 5, 1183, Monreale became an archiepiscopal see. This is not the place to deal with the political and ecclesiastical quarrels that prompted the king to lavish so much honor and money on Monreale, but anyone approaching the place cannot but be impressed by the monumental building that dominates from its hill a whole landscape, still a symbol of the ambitions of its founder. The creation, alas, proved to be too personal. With William II the reign of the Hautevilles over Sicily came to an end, and it was Palermo, not Monreale, where the new rulers, the Hohenstaufens, were buried and where they lie in the cathedral in the same prophyry splendor as William's grandfather, Roger II.

• *The Cathedral.* Demus describes the building as late Norman and calls it a combination of Latin basilica and Greek cross-in-square church. However, the dome one would expect is missing. The unusual size of the church gives it special features. Its enormous walls provide a wonderful opportunity for mosaic decoration, of which full advantage has been taken, making of the cathedral, as the same author says, a tremendous "picture gallery."

• *The Mosaics.* Entering a huge building like Monreale, with its interior totally covered with mosaics, is itself an experience. The impression is stunning. Yet one must differentiate between the overwhelming aspect of the whole and the values of the mosaics as such. Much restoration has changed them; some have been restored with stucco and paint, and even the architecture of the building has been meddled with. Two fires in the beginning of the 19th century caused great damage to both building and mosaics. The restorations in the first half of the 19th century have especially affected the central square and its wings. Later restorations after 1870, to stabilize and fix the mosaics, have had a "stiffening" effect caused by the flattening of the surface. The charm mosaics normally exert through their liveliness, which is due to the slight difference in angle between one tessera and another and which can change the aspect of the whole within minutes by any change in the angle of the incident light, may in great part be lacking in the mosaics of Monreale; still, there is much to admire and much to be learned from them, not least from the iconography, which has been perpetuated despite the restorations.

The mosaics occupy a surface of 68,000 square feet; they cover the nave with its two side aisles, the central square with its wings, and the three apses with their ante-chapels.

The general plan of the mosaics is as follows:

The central apse (sanctuary) with the Pantocrator in the conch.
The two side apses and their ante-chapels with the figures and the stories of St. Peter and St. Paul.
The central square (used as choir) and its wings with the Christ cycles.
The nave with Old Testament scenes.
The aisles south and north of the nave with the miracles of Christ.

[ON OPPOSITE PAGE] *Monreale: central apse*

• *Central Apse.* A stern Pantocrator in the conch, surrounded in the arch by nine medallions: at top, Christ Emmanuel (Matt. 1:23 and Isa. 7:14), at each side four prophets: in descending order, left, David, Elijah, Daniel, Nathan; right, Solomon, Samuel, Gideon, Elisha.

Below the conch, upper row: Virgin with Child, flanked by one archangel and six Apostles at each side (spreading over, left and right, on walls and piers); lower row: at each side seven saints, also spreading out left and right of apse.

• *Side Apses.* In the conch of the left (north) chapel, St. Paul enthroned; on the walls, some of the main events of his life.

In the conch of the right (south) chapel, St. Peter enthroned; on the walls, some of the main events in his life and the miracles of his healings.

• *Central Square (choir) and its Wings.* In addition to the various biblical scenes that fill the walls of the central square and its wings, there are innumerable medallions and portraits on the walls and in the arches. Among the portraits should be noted especially the two mosaics on the northeast and southeast piers of the central square showing the donor, William II, in the one being crowned by Christ, in the other offering the church to the Virgin. Further to be noted in the arches of the central square are a number of medallions portraying the ancestors of Christ (Matt. 1:1–16) and three other personages, Melchisedec, Enoch, and Noah.

In describing the walls above the arches of the central square and the walls of its wings, we follow the images on each of the walls separately, although in some cases the story may continue from one wall to another, as the visitor will readily detect for himself.

The arches of the central square and its wings are devoted to New Testament scenes, from the Annunciation, through the life of Christ, to Pentecost. The walls over and around the tops of the arches, looking from the central square to the south, west and north, show (always from left to right):

Central Square—South Wall

TOP TIER: The annunciation to Zachariah (Luke 1:11–17), Zachariah leaving the temple, the Annunciation to the Virgin, the Visitation (Mary and Elizabeth; Luke 1:39 ff.).

LOWER TIER, *around top of arch:* Joseph's dream, the flight into Egypt.

Monreale: northeast pier, with mosaic of William II crowned by Christ

Central Square—West Wall

TOP TIER: Nativity (in four panels).

LOWER TIER: The presentation in the temple, Christ among the doctors.

Central Square—North Wall

TOP TIER: Two mosaics of the Magi, Herod's order, the Massacre of the Innocents.

LOWER TIER: The miracle of turning water into wine (marriage at Cana; John 2:1–11), the baptism of Christ.

South Wing—South Wall

TOP TIER: The three temptations of Christ.

SECOND TIER: Christ and the Samaritan woman, the Transfiguration, the raising of Lazarus, two disciples bringing the ass.

THIRD TIER: The washing of the feet, the agony in the garden, the betrayal of Judas.

South Wing—West Wall
TOP TIER: The healing of the paralytic, the healing of the blind.
SECOND TIER: The entry into Jerusalem, the Last Supper.
THIRD TIER: The judgment of Pilate.

North Wing—West Wall
TOP TIER: The preparation of the cross, the Crucifixion.
SECOND TIER: The holy women at the sepulchre, *Noli me tangere*
(Christ appearing to Mary Magdalene, John 20:17).
THIRD TIER: Doubting Thomas.

North Wing—North Wall
TOP TIER: The descent from the cross, the burial of Christ, the harrowing of Hell.
SECOND TIER: The story of Emmaus (in four parts).
THIRD TIER: The miraculous draught of fishes, the Ascension, Pentecost.

• *The Nave.* The two sides of the nave are filled with Old Testament scenes placed in two rows, the lower between the arches, the higher between the windows. They are tied together by the two upper rows on the west wall.

Upper Row
SOUTH WALL: Scenes of the Creation, Adam in Paradise.
WEST WALL: The creation of Eve and her presentation to Adam.
NORTH WALL: Eve and the serpent, the expulsion from Paradise, Adam and Eve working, the sacrifice of Cain and Abel, Cain's curse, Lamech slaying Cain, Noah ordered to build the ark.

Lower Row
SOUTH WALL: Continuation of the story of Noah; building of the Tower of Babel, the hospitality of Abraham (Gen. 18:1–8).
WEST WALL: Lot and the angels, the destruction of Sodom.
NORTH WALL: Sacrifice of Isaac, Rebecca watering the camels, Rebecca's journey, Isaac and Rebecca, Isaac sending out Esau, Isaac blessing Jacob, Jacob's dream, and Jacob wrestling with the angel.

The bottom row of mosaics on the west wall, either side of the door, does not belong to the Old Testament cycle but is devoted to St. Castrense, whose relics were given to William II as a present on the occasion of his marriage with Joan of England in 1177.

• *The Aisles.* The south and north aisles of the nave continue the episodes from the life of Christ started in the south

Monreale: mosaic in nave, showing the building of the Tower of Babel

Below, *mosaic in north aisle of nave, showing Christ driving the money-changers from the temple*

wing, showing especially the healing scenes on the north and south walls.

From the foregoing it should be clear that the main iconography of the cathedral is systematically arranged and easy to follow, despite the scattered profusion of figures and medallion portraits of saintly persons, especially in the eastern part of the monument.

"The decoration of Monreale is a homogeneous work of art conceived by one leading artist in its main outlines and executed by a number of artists and workmen under a uniform direction." This view, which Demus bases on elaborate stylistic arguments, is borne out by the systematic arrangement of the whole program, which appears to be the consequence of a firm leadership and consistent execution within a comparatively short period.

Yet the construction evidently took some time. Demus considers the mosaics of the main apse and central presbytery as the earliest, then come those of the central square, the miracles of Christ in the side aisles, and the mosaics of the nave. Later came the side apses with their presbyteries, together with the mosaics of the wings on the inner walls and the scenes in the bottom tiers.

In all this should be kept in mind the frequent restorations, which nevertheless left the iconography intact.

     • *The Bronze Doors.* There are two pairs of bronze doors in the cathedral, that at the north side entrance, made by Barisanus of Trani, and that of the great west side portal, by Bonannus of Pisa, both executed 1186.

Diehl (*Manuel d'art byzantin*) points out how much both these Italian doors differ from their Byzantine predecessors, considering the Barisanus door with its twenty-eight compartments far superior to the Bonannus door. The compartments of the Barisanus door, still influenced by Eastern style, are surrounded by medallions of secular Byzantine-type subjects; two of them also depict secular subjects, the others containing saints (among them Byzantine saints), and two evangelical scenes: the Deposition from the Cross and the Descent of Christ into Hell, also Byzantine. Notwithstanding their Italian origin, the doors can be called Byzantine and Eastern, Barisanus evidently having worked from Greek examples in ivory or other materials.

The doors of Bonannus are totally different. The subjects on the one side are biblical scenes, from the creation of man to the history of Gideon; those on the other, evangelical scenes, from the Annunciation to the Death of the Virgin. None shows the finesse of the Barisanus work. The doors may remind one only remotely of Byzantium and are coarse in execution.

• *The Cloisters.* The wealth of sculptured capitals on the innumerable columns of the cloisters must for the greater part have been executed in William II's time. Their iconography is closely related to the mosaics of the cathedral. Some of the sculptures deal with the king—William offering the cathedral to the Virgin, the king enthroned, looking like a Byzantine emperor—but most are devoted to the New as well as the Old Testament.

We see: the expulsion from Paradise, Daniel and the lions, the Annunciation, the angel with Joseph, the Visitation, the Magi, the Good Shepherd, the holy women at the tomb, the Descent into Hell.

In addition to these, there are many secular scenes and lively animal motives, including the peacock, which in this period has become ornamental rather than symbolic.

The columns themselves with their oriental mosaic decoration and the little fountain with its oriental features add to the charm of the cloisters by showing that mixture of styles so typical for Sicily.

THE PORPHYRY TOMBS

THE TOMBS OF THE NORMAN KINGS in Sicily are in fact signs of a new dynastic yearning for greatness and splendor; as porphyry was a Byzantine symbol of imperial stature taken over by the popes of Rome for their sarcophagi, it must have appealed to Roger II even though it was the symbol of his adversaries.

Roger II donated two porphyry sarcophagi to his church of Cefalù, one to hold his own remains and one not intended for any definite person. As he was the first crowned king of Sicily, he thus from the beginning identified the glamor of porphyry with the royal title.

Trying to rule after one's death is always tricky. Roger II was buried not in Cefalù but in the cathedral of Palermo, and not in the porphyry tomb he had destined for himself. Choice of the burial place of the royal family became a violent source of controversy

Monreale: sculptured capitals in cloisters, showing above, William II *offering his church to the Virgin, and* below, Daniel in the lions' den

between Palermo, Cefalù, and Monreale. As a result, the present situation is that, of the royal persons buried in porphyry tombs, we find four in the Cathedral of Palermo—Roger II (d. 1154), Henry VI (d. 1197), Constance (daughter of Roger II and wife of Henry VI; d. 1198), and her son Frederick II (d. 1250)—and the fifth, William I (d. 1166), in the south transept of the Cathedral of Monreale. The remains of William II (d. 1189), founder of Monreale, lie in the Cathedral, not in a porphyry sacrophagus but in a much later tomb (1575).

The death dates of the royal persons so buried do not, however, correspond with the dates of construction of the tombs. Thus we find Roger II buried in a simple unadorned porphyry tomb, in which he was laid "provisionally." The Empress Constance lies in a porphyry tomb "glued together from as many as fourteen parts," as Prof. Deér informs us (*The Dynastic Porphyry Tombs of the Norman Period*); its style is based on the two Cefalù tombs modelled after a Roman Classic porphyry tomb. The remains of Henry VI, who ousted Roger's house of the Hautevilles, and those of his son Frederick II, ironically enough, rest in the two original Cefalù tombs.

The "temporary" tomb of Roger II is of the utmost simplicity, those of Constance and Henry VI (like that of William I in Monreale, which is a copy of Henry's tomb) have little adornment. Only the tomb of Frederick II has more elaborate decorations. The Palermo porphyry tombs all have canopies, the Monreale does not.

PIANA DEGLI ALBANESI

WHILE THE COMING of the Normans meant a general decline of the Orthodox faith in former Byzantine Italy, there were exceptions and in some places Orthodoxy remained alive into the 15th and 16th centuries. At the time that it seemed doomed in Southern Italy, a sudden revival occurred. When, after the gallant struggle of the colorful Albanian hero Scanderbeg (d. 1467), his country was gradually lost to the Turks, a great many Christian refugees from Albania as well as from the Peloponnesus came to Italy. Most of them settled in Sicily and Southern Italy, keeping their language and their customs. These people to a great extent continued to follow the Orthodox rites, thus reinforcing the remnants of their faith they had found in the South, although they gradually came to accept papal supremacy.

Such a community, among several others round about it, is the Piana degli Albanesi, which lies in the rolling hill-country back of Palermo. Though there may be no Byzantine monuments to be sought out there, attending a service in the Church of St. Demetrius or in the square before it brings one a most rewarding experience; for here the Italo-Byzantine Greek chants are to be heard, especially at Easter, on Epiphany, on the name-day of St. George (April 23), and at celebrations for the Madonna Hodegetria (Tuesday after Pentecost and September 2).

Piana degli Albanesi: service in the piazza before the church

PIAZZA ARMERINA

SOUTH OF ENNA, which is situated east of the center of the island, is the village of Piazza Armerina. Though the floor mosaics (covering an immense surface of 3,500 square meters and dating from

Piazza Armerina: floor mosaic of rhinoceros

around 300) in the ruins of the great Roman villa nearby are neither
Byzantine nor Christian art, they are of interest to the Byzantine-
oriented visitor because they are contemporary with many frescoes
in the catacombs and with the floor mosaics of the Cathedral
of Aquileia in Northern Italy (constructed between 314 and 320).
Nor are they too far in time from the 4th/5th-century mosaics we see
in S. Pudenziana and S. Costanza in Rome or in the Chapel of S.
Aquilino in Milan.

Though the original purpose of the villa is a matter of dispute,
its size and importance would point to an imperial residence. It is
generally considered to have been the hunting lodge of the imperial
family of Maximinianus Herculius (co-emperor of Diocletian, 284–
305) who, in the territorial division between the two, was respon-
sible for Italy and Africa—a combination that tallies well with the
subjects of the mosaics, which in their elaborate hunting scenes
show the late classic style of Italy as well as many African animals,
such as lions, elephants, rhinos, and ostriches.

Ss. Maria e Donato, Murano: detail of mosaic of Virgin in apse

VI

BYZANTINE ASPECTS OF NORTHERN ITALY

MILAN

THE CITY OF MILAN played a great role in late Roman history, especially in matters concerning the Christian church, and hence in the formation of Byzantium. Its name will forever be linked with the meeting of Constantine and Licinius in 313, for there it was that they are assumed, rightly or wrongly, to have decided on a policy of toleration toward the Christians (p. 19). The famous St. Ambrose (339–97) became bishop of Milan in 374. He exercised a great influence on the formulation of Christian belief; from him St. Augustine received the basis of his Christian doctrine.

In Milan we find two examples of the rare early Christian mosaics in existence, in the Chapel of S. Aquilino in the Church of S. Lorenzo (closing 4th or early 5th century) and those in the small mor-

145

tuary chapel of S. Vittore in Ciel d'Oro in the Church of S. Ambrogio (late 5th century).

      Chapel of S. Aquilino. In two of its conches opposite the entrance door, the Chapel of S. Aquilino has two highly interesting mosaics, both done in rather pallid colors. The one on the right shows Christ with Apostles, and it is the young beardless Christ as teacher, an interpretation normal to the early period of the mosaic. The one on the left (partly destroyed), showing a shepherd with his sheep, suggests the Good Shepherd, though the iconography is so different in this case that it may rather suggest a representation of the shepherds in the Nativity—or simply a non-Biblical landscape with shepherds and sheep. The dark figure on the right may be a prophet—perhaps Elijah, since in the upper part of the picture there are faint indications of the fiery chariot with its horses ascending (a 4th-century fresco in the catacombs of the Via Latina in Rome shows the same combination of Elijah with a shepherd and sheep). In such mosaics as this one and the one in the pre-Constantinian necropolis under S. Pietro in Rome, one may also think of Christ-Helios, Christ the Light of the World.

      In the atrium to the chapel are some remains of mosaics.

Chapel of S. Aquilino, Milan: Christ as teacher, with disciples

S. Ambrogio, Milan: section of apse mosaic

S. Ambrogio. The Basilica of S. Ambrogio, founded by him in 385, rebuilt 789–859 in Romanesque Lombard style, and again restored in 1098–1128, contains a big apse mosaic of the late 12th century showing Christ enthroned and the death of St. Ambrose. Though well composed, this mosaic has a certain stiffness.

• *S. Vittore in Ciel d'Oro.* To the right of the apse is the small mortuary chapel of S. Vittore in Ciel d'Oro, showing St. Victor, a Milanese martyr, within a wreath in the cupola. On the walls we see St. Ambrose between Sts. Gervase and Protase, and St. Maternus between Sts. Nabor and Felix. The two last-named, natives of Mauretania, were martyred at Laus Pompeia (the present Lodi, south of Milan) and buried in Milan. Though of Moorish origin, they are not represented as Moors.

The chapel and its mosaics are probably of the 5th century, though some have suggested the 6th century. Many mosaics have disappeared, but those remaining are in good condition and are very much worth visiting.

Chapel of S. Vittore in Ciel d'Oro, Milan: mosaics of Sts. Ambrose and Nabor

THE FRESCOES OF
S. MARIA DI CASTELSEPRIO

AFTER ABOUT AN HOUR'S RUN on the road from Milan to Varese (and some twenty minutes before Varese), one turns off the highway to the right, at Torba en Val Olona, near Tradate, along a country road. The ruins of Castelseprio very soon come in sight: the remnants of a castle (probably 5th/6th-century), the Basilica of S. Giovanni Battista of about the same period and the baptistery with its double baptismal font, the Church of S. Paolo, and some secular buildings.

The main objective of the Byzantine-oriented traveler, however, is a visit to the tiny church of S. Maria di Castelseprio or Foris Portas, which stands in a grove of trees a little distance to the left as one approaches the ruins (the key at the guardian's house).

According to Prof. Kurt Weitzmann (*The Fresco Cycle of S. Maria di Castelseprio*), it was only in 1944 that a whitewash covering was removed and so there came to light frescoes "that show a style without parallel on Italian soil, and [that] in artistic as well as historical importance rank with the great discoveries of our century, comparable in quality to the mosaics of the Hagia Sophia in Constantinople."

A *graffito* found on the paint of one of the frescoes mentions Ardericus, who was Archbishop of Milan between the years 938 and 945, and this leads Professor Weitzmann to the conclusion (backed also by convincing stylistic arguments) that the date of the frescoes must be around the middle of the 10th century. In this, Weitzmann rejects the thesis of an Italian scholar, Capitani d'Arzago, that it should be toward the end of the 7th century, a time when many artists from the East fled to Italy—which in d'Arzago's view would explain the Eastern character of the paintings.

In any case, the mingling of classic and Eastern features and the excellent execution of the frescoes produces, despite their pale, much-faded coloring, an effect of delicate beauty and high artistic value. (It is well to see them on a day of good light.) The profiles of the Virgin, the angels, and the Salomé, in the scene of the Nativity, are well and finely drawn; the fiery old priest in the trial by water, the good Joseph in the journey to Bethlehem, the moving old Simeon in the Presentation in the Temple, the gay kings in the Adoration of the Magi are all rare works of art.

The east wall of the church has two zones of paintings with three windows, above the middle one of which is a painting of Christ.

UPPER ZONE: *left to right,* the Annunciation and part of the Visitation, the trial by water (Book of James, or Protoevangelium XV and XVI; also Num. 5:11--29), Christ, Joseph's dream, the journey to Bethlehem.

LOWER ZONE: *left to right (following two frescoes of which very little remains),* the Presentation in the Temple, the Nativity (for Salomé helping the midwife, see Book of James XIX:2 and XX, and Pseudo-Matthew XIII), linking up with the annunciation to the shepherds.

Finally, on the inner side of the triumphal arch we find the Adoration of the Magi, while above the arch appears the empty throne (Etimasia) of the Last Judgment, flanked by two angels.

RAVENNA

AT FIRST BLUSH, Ravenna may seem rather disappointing. The town itself has very little charm left. Its beauty, well conserved, is inside the buildings—but such beauty!

Ravenna had a remarkable history. Its situation in the marshes formed by the rivers flowing into the Adriatic made it a safe retreat, as we have seen (p. 21), for the Western emperor Honorius (395–423), who took over after the death of his father Theodosius the Great (379–95), and also for his sister Galla Placidia during her guardianship for her son Valentine III (425–55). Its situation near the sea made it, furthermore, a prosperous port.

Theodoric, King of the Ostrogoths (d. 526), who officially governed as vassal of Byzantinum—though Byzantine influence was formal only—followed Honorius' example of residing in Ravenna. Theodoric also had a Byzantine background, having, as a youngster, been sent by his father to Constantinople as a pledge of an alliance with the Eastern emperor Leo. After Justinian the Great had made Italy part of the Empire again, it was from Ravenna that those areas of the country not lost to the Lombards were governed until these also were lost (p. 24).

Ravenna's artistic history—from the first half of the 5th century, during the time of Galla Placidia and Theodoric, to the 6th century when Justinian reconquered Italy—was therefore always connected with the Eastern Roman Empire. No wonder that Charles Diehl, in his small volume on the subject, says that in Ravenna, "better than in the East, better than in Constantinople itself or in Salonica can one study the Byzantine art of the 5th and 6th centuries," even though in the post-Justinian period Byzantium's position there hardly enabled the city to remain a center of much artistic activity.

The visitor to Ravenna will find that its Byzantine works of art spread over four different periods. This allows him to study, concentrated here in one town, four different periods in the style-development of Byzantine wall mosaics. These periods are those of:

1. Galla Placidia (mosaics between 430 and 458)
2. Theodoric (mosaics between 526 and 534)
3. Justinian (mosaics between 534 and 569)
4. The 7th century

Mausoleum of Galla Placidia: mosaic of the Good Shepherd

Mausoleum of Galla Placidia. The great mosaics of Galla Placidia's time are those in the Mausoleum that bears her name, built before 450, and in the Baptistery of the Orthodox, built between 449 and 458. The motives used in the mosaics are, of course, characteristic of this early period. Inside the mausoleum we see, in the lunette above the entrance, Christ, beardless, as the Good Shepherd. In the lunette opposite, St. Lawrence holding cross and book, at his left the grate, instrument of his martyrdom, and further left, a chest containing the four Gospels. Under the cupola, in the left upper lunette, a mosaic of Sts. Peter and Paul, reminding us of the 4th/5th-century apse mosaic in S. Costanza in Rome (p. 49); in each of the other three lunettes, two Apostles, all looking up at the Cross in the center of the cupola with its symbols of the four Evangelists. The interior of the Mausoleum is further covered by graceful mosaic decorations with motives of plants, flowers, fruits, and birds. Three sarcophagi inside the Mausoleum are supposed to contain the remains of Galla Placidia and members of her family.

Baptistery of the Orthodox. Like the Mausoleum, the Baptistery of the Orthodox, also of Galla Placidia's time, is richly decorated with mosaics that cover almost the whole interior. The center of the dome shows Christ being baptized, surrounded by the twelve Apostles. In the circle around the latter, we find the four Gospel books and four representations of the empty throne of the Last Judgment (Ps. 9:8), on which lies the book with seven seals (Rev. 5:1). It seems that this symbol of the preparation of the throne (Etimasia), frequently used in later mosaics, appears here for the first time.

Baptistery of the Arians. The period of Theodoric is brought to us by part of the mosaics of S. Apollinare Nuovo (around 526) and the Baptistery of the Arians of the same period. This latter is in fact a duplication of the Baptistery of the Orthodox but, being of a different period, is different in style. Moreover it is rigid and lacks the charm of its earlier model.

S. Apollinare Nuovo. The famous mosaics in S. Apollinare Nuovo are among the most beautiful in existence. Of the three superimposed rows on the sides of the nave, the upper two belong to Theodoric's time. The middle row shows, between the

S. Apollinare Nuovo: south side of nave, with mosaic of Palace of Theodoric

windows against a golden background, saints, prophets and Apostles. The top row consists of small panels showing miracles and the Passion of Christ.

The lowest row is of Justinian's time and shows a long procession on the one side of saintly men, on the other of saintly women, all bearing martyrs' crowns, the two processions leaving the towns of Ravenna and Classis (its port) respectively. These mosaics of the lowest row suggest a completion or alteration of existing mosaics of Theodoric's time, with intent to obliterate all memories of that period; in fact, one can still see here and there remnants of figures that have disappeared.

S. Vitale. The church of S. Vitale is an outstanding example of the artistic activities of Justinian's epoch. This church, which is all covered with mosaics and marble, has few counterparts in Byzantine art.

In the apse one sees the donor, the bishop Ecclesius, with a little model of his church, a type of subject later to become so

S. Apollinare in Classe: apse mosaic, symbolizing the Transfiguration

S. Vitale: mosaic of the Empress Theodora with her attendants

familiar. Opposite stands St. Vitalis, to whom the church is dedicated. In the center, Christ, seated on the globe, is represented still in the old manner, without a beard. Left, the sacrifice of Abraham and Abraham's hospitality; right, offerings of Abel and Melchisedec (Gen. 4:4 and 14:18); further to the left and right in the apse, the imperial groups: left, the emperor Justinian, with Bishop Maximian and followers (detail on p. 16), and right, the empress Theodora with her following, all in full Byzantine splendor.

S. Apollinare in Classe. Also of Justinian's time, San Apollinare in Classe has in its apse a mosaic in which two iconographic compositions are set in one. Framed in a circle of blue sky flaked with golden stars, a large gem-studded cross, symbolic of the Transfiguration, bears at the intersection of its arms the face of Christ. Above the cross appears the Hand of God. The cross is flanked by the figures of Moses and Elijah, usual in Transfiguration scenes, and below these, three sheep represent the Apostles Peter, James, and Paul, also traditional in this iconography.

The lower part of the mosaic shows an idyllic landscape that may represent Paradise, with St. Apollinaris *orans* between two rows of sheep symbolizing the Apostles.

Above the arch of the conch, again sheep are shown coming out of Jerusalem and Bethlehem, and above that again we see Christ with the symbols of the four Evangelists.

The mosaics between the windows and left and right on the lower part of the arch are, however, an example of the fourth period of the Ravenna mosaics, around 677. It is interesting to note that while the names of the bishops between the windows are given in Latin, those of the archangels Michael and Gabriel at the left and right are in Greek letters.

Among the sarcophagi that stand in the right nave, that of the 5th century containing the remains of the Archbishop Theodore should be noted.

The Archiepiscopal Palace. In the museum of the Archiepiscopal Palace is the famous 6th-century ivory bishop's chair or throne with carved plaques, all presenting biblical figures and stories. The Byzantine style of these reliefs is generally considered to be related to that of Syria and Egypt.

S. Apollinare in Classe:
5th-century sarcophagus

Archiepiscopal Palace:
6th-century ivory bishop's
chair

The Justinian period has also left us a very unusual mosaic in the Archiepiscopal Chapel, a mosaic now restored but upon the original pattern: Christ as Warrior, stepping on a dragon and a snake (Ps. 91:13) and above, in the vault, birds on a background of golden tesserae.

After Justinian's death this vault was further decorated with mosaics, which provide us with another example of the fourth period of Ravenna's Byzantine art. Four angels hold the monogram of Christ, the two intersecting crosses; between the angels, the four symbols of the Evangelists. The arches are filled with medallions of Apostles and male and female saints. All these later mosaics —later 7th century?—show how rapidly this art was declining in Ravenna.

A visit to Ravenna is the more interesting because the mosaics are to be seen in an environment that retains many details of its Byzantine character—capitals of columns, various sculptures—notwithstanding all the destruction of war and of time itself.

VENICE AND SURROUNDINGS

VENICE STARTED OUT as a Byzantine province, protected from the barbarians by its lagoons; because of its safe abode, the city developed a great feeling of independence from Byzantium. In the 7th century it became a military province under Ravenna. From the end of that century it was ruled by doges, at first appointed by the emperor, later elected locally but confirmed by the emperor; and finally it became a hereditary ducal monarchy. In 774-75 it became an episcopal see. Enfeoffed by Charlemagne in 804, it was soon thereafter retaken by Byzantium, only to be recaptured by Charlemagne's son Pepin. In 812 the Byzantine emperor recognized Charlemagne as *imperator,* and as a *quid pro quo* Venice came back to the Byzantine fold. In all this competition between the two emperors, the tactical position of Venice became stronger. Because of its safe location, its growing commercial and financial power, and its tendency to be not over-scrupulous in its acts, Venice must have been an uneasy partner for the Byzantines; they tried to keep their hold on it by flexible arrangements and constant political and economic concessions, the latter leading in 1082 to the famous

Venetian trade monopoly in Constantinople.

The Byzantines made a pact with Venice in 1149 for help in combating the Normans of Sicily; but in 1151 this was broken by the Venetians, who furthermore sided with the Hungarians against Byzantium. This insolence led to the seizure of all Venetian property in Constantinople by the Byzantine emperor in 1171. In 1175 the Venetians sided with Sicily against Byzantium, but this war turned out badly for them and in 1176 they had to make peace. The relationship did not improve with time. Their cunning and their financial strength at last enabled the Venetians to turn the Fourth Crusade (1204) into the raid on Constantinople that resulted in so much booty for Venice. Although it was Venice's rival Genoa that helped Byzantium reconquer Constantinople (1261) when the Crusaders proved ineffective governors, the Venetians nevertheless managed to regain their former position there.

Despite their uneasy relationship, Byzantium and Venice seemed to belong together; connections were maintained under the Paleologian dynasty of Byzantium (1261–1453) until the bitter end, an end that also meant the beginning of the decline of Venetian power. The ties between the two also appear in the fact that, even after the fall of Constantinople, many Greeks fleeing from the Turks came to Venice. There they must have felt at home, establishing a Greek quarter near the Ponte dei Greci, where the Orthodox church of S. Giorgio dei Greci still functions and where one finds the museum of Byzantine icons made in Venice after Byzantium itself had disappeared.

It is clear that the constantly changing relationship between Byzantium and Venice also impinged on the development of Byzantine style in the latter city, and this complicates the understanding of "Byzantine" monuments there. Natural though it was that Venetian Byzantine art should show a general trend toward Westernization, this was sometimes interrupted by a resurgence of direct Byzantine influence, even after Venetian workshops working in Byzantine style replaced that influence.

It was also through Venice that Byzantine art reached the rest of Italy, as was the case when Pope Honorius III asked the doge Pietro Giani around 1220 to sent Venetian artists to set up the apse mosaic in the Basilica of S. Paolo fuori le Mura in Rome, where we now see Christ blessing *alla greca* (p. 68). As a result of the historical events affecting the relations between Byzantium and Venice, we shall, when studying the great Basilica of S. Marco, be dealing with Byzantine monuments of varied origin, namely those imported from Constantinople, those made for the church under direct Byzantine influence, and those carried out in Venice in the Venetian Byzantine manner.

S. Marco

• *The Building.* The present church was started in 1063 and was probably consecrated in 1095. It is of brick, in the form of a Greek cross with five cupolas, in principle a Byzantine form.

The first view every visitor gets is that of the west, the principal facade, now Gothic in style, so much altered and added to in the course of the years that it scarcely suggests the original conception of the building. This can be checked on the spot by studying the mosaic in the facade's leftmost arch. Constructed in 1267, this mosaic shows the simple exterior of the S. Marco of that time. To take in the grandeur of the building one should examine it from various sides; a look from the neighboring quiet courtyard of the Palazzo Ducale reveals its simple beauty.

Apart from architectural changes and additions, S. Marco has been adorned by an enormous number of works of art, many of which have little to do with the building itself. Some are of great importance in themselves, and in many cases owe their preservation only to the fact that they formed part of the loot from the sack of Constantinople in 1204.

For reasons already explained, the various origins of the Byzantine-related monuments we find here, the various periods of their construction, and the various influences they were subjected to often make them very difficult to analyze. They have become the subject of many scholarly and highly intriguing discussions.

THE WEST FACADE: There are a number of mosaics on the west facade, the one on the extreme left, mentioned above, being the only one that is Byzantine. It is 13th-century (1267) and depicts the arrival at the church of the remains of St. Mark, brought back from Alexandria by the Venetians. It shows the famous Greek horses standing as they do today.

It also shows six sculptured plaques between the spandrels of the arches. Of the six, four were made in Venice and two imported, one of these latter being classic, the other Byzantine. They are related as pairs: nos. 1 and 6, 2 and 5, 3 and 4. They represent, left to right:

1. Heracles carrying the Erymanthian boar (6th century B.C.; Classic)
2. Virgin *orans* (Venetian-Byzantine)
3. St. George (Venetian-Byzantine)
4. St. Demetrius (Byzantine, late 12th century; brought among the spoils from Constantinople)
5. Archangel Gabriel (Venetian-Byzantine)
6. Heracles carrying the Ceryneian hind, his left foot on the Lernean hydra (matching no. 1, but made in Venice)

The Venetian-made sculptures may all be dated 12th/13th century.

S. Marco: relief of St. Demetrius, on west facade

The central porch of the west facade has, over its 11th-century bronze doors with lion heads, three concentric arches decorated with a wealth of sculpture that, though based on Byzantine and Islamic motives, was much influenced by the budding Romanesque style. The visitor, who may be deterred by the modern mosaic of the triumph of Christ under the uppermost and largest of them, will do well to devote his time to the arches themselves, in Romanesque Byzantine style.

Under the first, immediately above the entrance door, is the Romanesque sculpture of the dream of St. Mark, who reclines asleep, an angel standing behind him. On the front of this arch the activities of men from youth to old age are shown; in the soffit, Earth, Ocean, animals. On the front of the middle arch, virtues and beatitudes according to the Sermon on the Mount (Matt. 5:3–11); in the soffit, the months of the year. On the front of the top arch, which frames the modern mosaic, Christ and prophets, and in the soffit, the professions of men.

The dominating monument of the west facade is that of the four Classic Greek horses of gilded bronze (4th/3rd century B.C.), standing on the loggia above the arches. In themselves, they are worth a trip to Venice. They are said to have been brought from the island of Chios to adorn the Hippodrome in Constantinople. The Venetians in their turn carted them off to their city as an acquisition from the Fourth Crusade. Later, they again caught the fancy of a conqueror: Napoleon took them to Paris. They did not stay there long, and, except for a short absence from Venice for their protection during the Second World War, they have stood where we now see them ever since.

THE NORTH FACADE: This facade shows a number of unrelated plaques, most of which are intended merely as decoration. The relief of Alexander the Great being borne to heaven by griffons, a representation of pride, is considered to be Romanesque (probably 12th century). It is a subject that appeared in Italy at that period; we meet it in, for example, the priest Pantaleon's floor mosaics (dated 1163–66) in the Cathedral of Otranto (p. 110).

The sacrifice of Isaac, to the left of it, is probably from a Venice workshop.

The reliefs of Christ and the Evangelists on the west and north sides of the Capella dei Mascoli are Byzantine (12th/13th century).

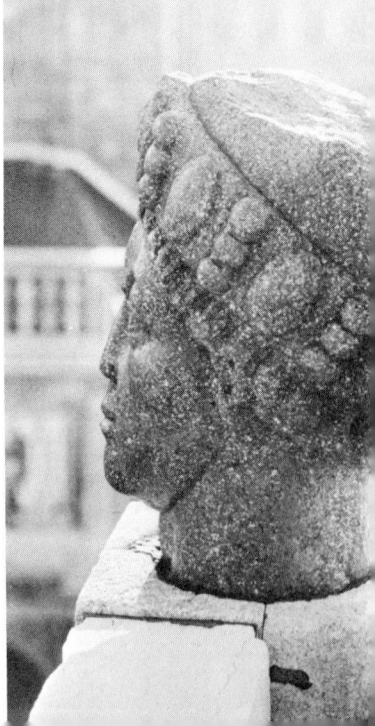

S. Marco: "*Pilastri d'Acri,*" on southwest facade; below left, *porphyry group of emperors,* on southwest corner; below right, *porphyry head, on southwest corner of balustrade of loggia*

It would seem that they were transferred at some time from the iconostasis to the north facade.

THE SOUTH FACADE: The porphyry group built into the base of the southwest corner of the Treasury, each pair in affectionate embrace, comes from Byzantium. Volbach, in his book on early Christian art, dates it around 300 (holding the right pair to be Diocletian and Maximian, the left pair Galerius and Constantius I Chlorus). The group is surrounded by some imported plaques.

To the left of the group of emperors (before the closed door of the Treasury) are two magnificent free-standing Byzantine pillars, known as the "Pilastri d'Acri" since it has always been supposed that they were brought from Acre; on the basis of recent archeological excavations in Istanbul, however, they have now been identified as coming from the Church of Polyeuktos that once stood in Constantinople. They too must have formed part of the spoils of the Fourth Crusade. Over the Treasury door there are several interesting little circular Byzantine plaques.

A lovely unidentified porphyry Byzantine head is perched for no apparent reason on the southwest corner of the balustrade of the loggia of the horses. Below it there stands the "Pietra del Bando," possibly from Syria, the remainder of a column from which decrees were published.

• *Doors and Sculptures*

THE NARTHEX: Around the three sides of the west arm of the cross of the church runs a narthex, the west and north domes of which are adorned with mosaics (to be dealt with presently). The south arm of the narthex is closed off and taken up by the Chapel of Zeno (southwest corner) and the Baptistery, both of which are entered from inside the church.

One enters the church from the narthex through the central portal. The bronze doors of this entrance are copies of the doors to the right, the Porta di S. Clemente, which were made in Constantinople in the 11th century and may have been a gift of Emperor Alexius I Comnenus (1081–1118). The fourteen squares of either door, each portraying a saint, are worked with inlaid silver (like the doors, also made in Constantinople, given by the Pantaleone family to Amalfi, Atrani, Monte S. Michele, and S. Paolo fuori le Mura in Rome). The 12th-century sculpture all around, on capitals, arches, and so forth, should be noted.

THE INTERIOR: Inside the church one will find a number of bas-reliefs, often of the Madonna *orans*. Some of these bas-reliefs are Byzantine and were brought from Constantinople during the Fourth Crusade; others were made in Venice. Above the inside of the Porta di S. Clemente, for example, there is an *orans* taken to be 13th-century Venetian-Byzantine in style, and to the left of it, on the south wall, right of the door leading to the Baptistery, a Deesis (Christ flanked by the Virgin and John the Baptist) that is late 11th-century Byzantine, probably part of the spoils of 1204.

Right of the altar in the Capella della Madonna Nicopeia ("bringing victory") on the east side of the north transept, we find a Madonna with Christ child, and left of the altar, two saints, above them three busts, all of which are 11th/12th-century Byzantine and probably also part of the spoils.

Beside the entrance to the Capella dei Mascoli in the northwest corner of the north transept, there is a relief of the Madonna *orans*, probably Venetian-Byzantine.

Nearby on a pillar in the north aisle of the nave is another *orans*, probably of Byzantine origin; and on another nearby pillar a Venetian-Byzantine Madonna with Christ child: the Madonna dello Schioppo ("of the gun"), so called from the rifle (an ex-voto) attached to the wall beside it.

(For three reliefs in the Baptistery, which is not always open, see p. 169).

• *The Presbytery*

THE CIBORIUM: The columns of the ciborium raise one of the most controversial problems among art historians. Some argue that the two front pillars are 5th-century, brought from Constantinople after 1204, and that the two rear pillars are to be considered 13th-century Venetian. While others date all the pillars 13th-century, it is quite possible that they were all reworked in a Venetian workshop. Such workshops, apart from doing repairs and restoration, also created works in earlier styles, so that even iconographic arguments may not in this case have the value they otherwise have. Of the two front pillars, the left deals with the Nativity, the right with the death of Christ.

THE PALA D'ORO: Behind the altar, we find the Pala d'Oro, a precious, several-times-remodelled rectangular altarpiece of gold, silver, precious stones, and enamel plaques of various sizes. Its history is complicated. In its present Gothic form, the enamels and precious stones together provide a dazzling combination of beautiful objects. Each of its plaques deserves careful inspection.

A *pala* for S. Marco was first ordered in Constantinople in the 10th century. It is not certain whether this first *pala* formed the nucleus of the one set up by Doge Ordelaffo Falier in 1105. Later (1209), Doge Pietro Giani had it remodelled, and in the middle of the 14th century it received its present Gothic form, yet its character remains Byzantine.

The upper part of the *pala* shows a row of six plaques, three on either side of the archangel Michael, each representing a feast of the church: Palm Sunday (Entry into Jerusalem), Descent into Hell, Crucifixion, Ascension, Pentecost, Dormition of the Virgin. This upper row is thought to have been one of a series of twelve made for the Church of the Pantocrator in Constantinople in the 12th century, and brought to Venice after 1204. The little plaques and medallions that surround it are excellent examples of 10th- and 11th-century Byzantine work.

The lower part of the *pala* has a center which shows Christ enthroned surrounded by the four Evangelists, above him the empty throne of the Last Judgment (Etimasia) with a seraphim and an archangel on either side. Below Christ, the Virgin *orans*. To the right of the Virgin is the figure of Empress Irene, to the left that of the aforementioned Ordelaffo Falier, a strange combination indeed. Various explanations have been brought forward, among them that originally the portrait must have been that of the Emperor Alexius I Comnenus (1081–1118), Irene's husband, the name and the design of the head having been changed later. The design of the present head would indicate a somewhat rough alteration; the fact, however, that the costume does not indicate an imperial personage would point to a more complicated solution. The whole center of the lower *pala* may be dated 11th/12th century.

Left and right of the centerpiece of the lower panel are three rows of enamel plaques: in the upper row, angels; in the middle row, Apostles; in the lowest row, prophets. These three rows of plaques are, like the six plaques of the feasts in the upper portion, supposed to have been made in Constantinople in the 12th century and to have formed part of the loot of the Fourth Crusade. Of about the same period, but perhaps of Venetian origin, are the twenty-nine small rectangular plaques that surround the top and sides of this lower part, showing evangelical scenes and episodes of the life of St. Mark.

• *The Treasury (Tesoro).* A visit to the Treasury of S. Marco is highly to be recommended, especially after one has seen the glory of the Pala d'Oro. Objects such as those it houses are rare; they, too, belong in great part to the loot of 1204 and may thereby have escaped later destruction in the final fall of Constantinople.

One finds here the famous 6th/7th-century bishop's chair—which is, in fact, a reliquary—that, according to tradition, was given by Emperor Heraclius (610–41) to the Cathedral of Grado. Its sculptures show the Tree of Life, the Lamb, the Four Rivers of Life, and the symbols of the Evangelists.

Besides the various gold objects with their enamels and precious stones, one should not fail to study the four fine Byzantine *relievo* (embossed) icons, two (10th century) of the archangel Michael and two (12th/13th century) of the Crucifixion.

• *Mosaics in the Narthex.* Like all monuments in S. Marco, the Byzantine-related mosaics are of various periods, their artisans of various backgrounds. Such mosaics are to be found in the narthex and in the church itself.

THE NARTHEX: Left and right of the door leading from the narthex into the interior are early 12th-century mosaics of the Evangelists that belong among the oldest in the church, having been set up soon after construction of the present building. From left to right, they show Matthew, Mark, Luke, and John, beautiful against their golden background. Above them, and of the same period, there is a Madonna in a niche with three saints on either side, also in niches, with empty niches between.

The cupola mosaics of the narthex all deal with Old Testament scenes that are based on miniatures from the so-called Cotton Bible, a 6th-century manuscript (named after its owner, an English merchant) most of which has unfortunately since been destroyed by fire so that only a few fragments remain. The dates at which these mosaics were made gradually move up in time through the 13th century as one passes along the narthex as described below, and this gives one, despite the restorations and changes, an excel-

S. Marco: mosaics of the four Evangelists, to left and right of entrance door from narthex into church

lent opportunity to study the growing influence of Western style.

The series of the Old Testament stories starts in the south cupola of the west wing of the narthex. The south cupola itself shows the creation of the world and Adam in Paradise.

The first vault, moving to the north, shows stories of Noah; the second, Noah's death and the construction of the Tower of Babel.

The next cupola carries stories of the life of Abraham; in the lunette (east), the hospitality of Abraham, and, in the pendentives, medallions of Daniel, Jeremiah, Ezekiel, and Isaiah.

In the cupola of the northwest corner start the stories of the life of Joseph with, in the pendentives, medallions of Samuel, Elijah, Habakuk, Nathan.

The second cupola of the north wing of the narthex and its south lunette give more stories of the life of Joseph.

The third cupola and its south lunette continue the stories of Joseph. In the pendentives, medallions of the Evangelists.

The last (east) cupola, as well as the north half-cupola, shows the life of Moses. In the pendentives, Solomon, David, Zachariah, and Malachi. In the east half-cupola, the Madonna with Christ child, St. John, and St. Mark.

• *Mosaics Inside the Church.* After entering the church, one should turn around to see above the door a Venetian-Byzantine mosaic (1270) of Christ between the Virgin and St. Mark.

The five great domes or cupolas over the church itself needed a great many subjects to fill them. Their decoration, in consequence, though its subjects are Byzantine, breaks with Byzantine tradition governing their usual location.

THE WEST CUPOLA: The mosaic in the west cupola, set up in 1150, shows the familiar picture of the Pentecost (Acts 2), certainly Byzantine-inspired but also Romanesque in style and rather rigid if we compare it with the moving Pentecost mosaic of the Church of Hosios Lukas in Greece, which is a century earlier. In the center of the dome, we see the empty throne, with the Dove, and all around it the Apostles receiving the Holy Ghost. Between the windows in the drum, we see the converted peoples to whom they brought the Gospel, as mentioned in Acts 2:7–11. In the pendentives, four angels.

THE CENTRAL CUPOLA: The mosaic in the central cupola shows the Ascension, Christ being taken to Heaven by four angels;

in a circle around them, the Virgin between two angels, and the Apostles. Between the windows, the sixteen virtues of Christ. This 13th-century mosaic, though executed by Venetian artisans, is much nearer to Byzantine style than that of the west cupola. The four Evangelists in the pendentives were done over in the 19th century.

The mosaics of the lower part of the south and west arches that carry the central cupola should be noted here. They are taken from miniatures and have the character of fresco decorations: for example, in the south arch, the Temptation in the Desert (with its little devils), and right under it the Entry into Jerusalem. Those closest to the Byzantine conception of the festival icons are the Anastasis and the Crucifixion in the arch between the central and west cupolas (early 13th century).

THE EAST CUPOLA: The mosaic of the east cupola, above the presbytery, shows Christ, not as Pantocrator, but as Emmanuel (meaning "God with us"), which is unusual in Byzantine iconography. It is based on the prophecy of Isaiah (7:14), which is also referred to by Matthew (1:22–23). Christ, in the center, is 13th-century; the rest of the mosaic, 12th-century. Around him, with the Virgin between Isaiah and Daniel, eleven other prophets. In the pendentives, the four symbols of the Evangelists.

The main apse pictures Christ enthroned (done over around 1500). In the spaces between the windows, Sts. Nicholas, Peter, Mark, and Hermagoras (first Bishop of Aquileia), all probably 12th-century.

THE SOUTH CUPOLA: In the great south cupola, we see 13th-century mosaics of Sts. Leonard, Nicholas, Clement, and Blaise (S. Biagio).

THE NORTH CUPOLA: In the center of the great north cupola of St. John Evangelist, there is a Greek cross with passages from the Sermon on the Mount. It is surrounded by episodes from the life of John the Evangelist. Between the windows are the symbols of the Evangelists, among other motifs; in the pendentives, Sts. Jerome, Gregory, Augustine, Ambrose (13th century).

• *The Baptistery.* The mosaics of the Baptistery well deserve study. They are beautiful and interesting from a stylistic standpoint because, while still Byzantine-related, they represent, so to speak, the "last call" of Byzantium in S. Marco before the West took over. They are to be dated around the middle of the

14th century. Greek lettering is still much in evidence in them.

In the first cupola, Christ in Glory appears above the altar. Behind the altar are three reliefs: the Baptism of Christ, center, flanked by a lively St. George and a more clumsily portrayed St. Theodore. They belong to the same period as the Baptistery mosaics—examples, in other words, of sculpture made in the time of the Paleologian dynasty in Constantinople, the style of which still made itself felt outside Byzantium's shrunken borders, these three reliefs (with the possible exception of the St. Theodore) having been executed in Venice.

In the middle cupola, above the baptismal font, Christ is commanding the Apostles to baptize, and under this each Apostle is seen carrying out his mission, with the name of the place in which he did so. Note the interesting point that in the squinches appear four doctors of the Greek Orthodox Church, very well executed, an example of the Byzantine influence still active even at so late a date (St. Basil was done over in the 19th century).

The vault at the end of the Baptistery leading to the Chapel of Zeno shows scenes from the youth of Christ.

• *The Gallery.* A narrow structure running from one pillar to another in a not very logical manner, the gallery is reached by ascending the little staircase (right of the main entrance to the church from the narthex) leading to the horses and the museum; it allows the visitor to complete his picture of the church and to see some mosaics otherwise difficult to observe.

Walking along the south arm of the gallery before reaching the south transept, one sees on the soffit of an arch a 17th-century mosaic of Emperor Constantine and his mother Helena, showing how even in that very late period, after the disappearance of Byzantium itself, these two personages so important to the formation of the Byzantine Empire were remembered in Venice.

On the west wall of the south transept one can see from the gallery the mosaic (second half of 13th century) picturing the prayer that the lost relics of St. Mark may be retrieved and the miraculous opening, with the help of St. Mark himself, of the pillar in which they had been hidden.

From the north arm of the gallery, one can see in the west aisle of the north transept a great number of beautiful and interesting mosaics of the life of the Virgin (13th century), ranging from

Joseph's dream (Matt. 1:20, Protevangelium XIV:2) through the Annunciation and the Visitation to the journey to Bethlehem.

• *The Museum.* In the west side of the church, at about the level of the gallery and behind the loggia of the horses, is the museum.

It contains pieces of various periods, among them mosaics of the 13th/14th centuries, two 12th-century frontals made of Byzantine embroidery, one with an inscription showing it was a gift of Constantinus Comnenus, a cousin of the emperor Emanuel Comnenus (1143–80), and an icon of the Madonna, possibly of the 13th century.

Museum of Venetian-Greek Icons. In the middle of the 14th century many Byzantines, seeing the Turkish advances, fled from Byzantium, some of them settling in Venice, which they knew so well. It was not until 1470, however, that the Greek colonists were permitted to worship according to their own rites. A little later, in 1498, they were allowed to form a *confraternita* of their own, protected by their favorite saint, Nicholas. In 1526 they constructed their own church dedicated to St. George, now called S. Giorgio dei Greci. This Greek community continued as such and in the 16th and 17th centuries developed a Greek-Byzantine school of painting, which was active in decorating their church but also produced other religious paintings. These paintings have now been collected in a museum (under the auspices of the Istituto Ellenico de Studi Bizantini e post-Bizantini), next to the Greek Orthodox church near the Ponte dei Greci, not far behind S. Marco. The post-Byzantine icons brought together here show how Byzantium survived for a couple of centuries in Venice after it had ceased to exist as an empire.

Murano. On the island of Murano, easily reached by *vaporetto* from Venice and popular with tourists visiting the glass industry there, stands Ss. Maria e Donato, a brick Romanesque church founded much earlier but reconstructed in the 12th century. It shows Byzantine capitals and decorations. The floor is covered with geometrical patterns and various animals, some of fantastic nature. In the apse is a magnificent mosaic of the Virgin (early 13th century). The Madonna stands against a solid background of gold tesserae, without the Christ child, her hands raised (not her arms, as in most *orantes*). Under her, 13th-century frescoes of the Evangelists, which must have been done over later. The Virgin, drawn with utmost simplicity of line and simple in attitude and dress, shows a style so near to the style of the Torcello Virgin that the artists of the two apse mosaics may well have been the same.

Torcello. S. Maria Assunta, the cathedral of Torcello, another island not far from Venice, was founded around 640, re-built in the second half of the 9th century, and reconstructed in 1008.

The church was originally decorated with frescoes of the 11th century. The present Byzantine mosaics are of the 12th century (some place them a little earlier, some a little later).

In the apse stands the Virgin holding the Christ child, but otherwise alone and, as in Murano, against a glorious solid background of golden tesserae. Under her, the twelve Apostles. In the apse of the right aisle, Christ between the archangels Michael and Gabriel, with four saints; in the vault, four angels lifting the Lamb.

The west wall presents the formidable Last Judgment in its Orthodox iconography: above, the Descent into Hell flanked by

S. Maria Assunta, Torcello: mosaic of Virgin in apse

S. Maria Assunta, Torcello: mosaic of Last Judgment on west wall

five archangels. The row under this shows Christ in the *mandorla* (almond-shaped frame) between the Virgin and John the Baptist (the Deesis) with, left and right, the Apostles.

Underneath, the empty throne with the archangels, and animals spitting out the persons they have eaten. The fourth row shows at left the saved and at right those condemned, the bottom row depicting their subsequent fate. In all the scenes the artists have given free play to their fantasies, especially where Hell is pictured. We see at right of the fourth row the Devil with the Antichrist, looking deceptively innocent, on his lap (I John 2:18–22 and II John 7). Roundabout, heads of Christ's enemies, among them Mohammed. Bottom row, left, the eternal life of the saved souls and right, the terrors of Hell for the others. In the lunette just above the door, the Virgin *orans*.

S. Maria Assunta, Torcello: detail of Last Judgment, showing the Devil with the Antichrist on his lap

TRIESTE AND SURROUNDINGS

S. Giusto. The Byzantine interest of Trieste lies in the Cathedral of S. Giusto. The cathedral is a combination of two Romanesque churches, both of the 10th and 11th centuries, joined probably around 1300. On the floor in front of the presbytery are some remains of a 5th-century mosaic. The apse itself was rebuilt in 1842 and now has a modern mosaic in praise of which one may say that it does not try to imitate any older style and will not create any problems for future art historians. The two mosaics in the apses of the left and right aisles are very beautiful. In the right apse stands Christ with two martyrs protectors of the church, left, St. Justus, right, St. Servius (13th century). In the left apse, the Virgin with Archangels Michael and Gabriel (end of the 12th century); below, Apostles (early 13th century).

In this left chapel, under the mosaic, is exhibited an interesting icon of St. Justus, painted on silk. The ateliers of Venice having been so close to Byzantine techniques, it is possible that the icon may have been painted in Venice. The catalogue of the Byzantine Exhibition in Athens of 1964, where it was shown, calls it 12th/13th-century and says that although the lettering is Latin it is not excluded that the icon may have been executed in Byzantium for a Western client.

From Trieste one can easily visit Aquileia and neighboring Grado as well as Cividale. Nor should one resist the temptation to visit Poreč (the former Parenzo), in Yugoslavia, to see the interesting Basilica of Euphrasius with its beautiful 6th-century mosaics.

Aquileia. From early Christian days, Aquileia was a religious center that grew in importance; the seat of a patriarch, with St. Mark for its patron saint, it was once the envy of Venice. Even when in 828 the Venetians brought the mortal remains of St. Mark from Alexandria to Venice, that did not automatically entitle them to claim the Evangelist as their own patron saint, replacing Theodore Stratelates of Heraclea (sometimes identified with the warrior saint, Theodore Tiro; the former's attributes are a dragon and a sword, the latter's a lance and a crocodile, as he is shown on one of the columns in the Piazzetta on the Venetian waterfront). Only when Venice conquered and absorbed decaying Aquileia in 1420 was this aim achieved.

The Basilica of Aquileia still reflects the city's former greatness and history. It is constructed on the remains of a former 4th-century church, some lively floor mosaics of which can be seen on passing through the left side-door of the northwest corner inside the basilica. These floor mosaics bear testimony to the very early relation of Aquileia with Christianity. Even the present basilica, built by the

S. Giusto, Trieste: mosaic of right apse

Basilica of Aquileia: floor mosaic

great Bishop Poppo (1019–42) and consecrated in 1031, shows an elaborate floor mosaic of the 4th century.

The mosaic can be dated with certainty, as the dedicatory inscription in the central composition at the east end names the founder of the older church, Theodoros, Bishop of Aquileia (314–19). Considering that the Christians had only recently acquired freedom of religion in these years, the development of their church must have been rapid, even if the iconography of the floor with all its fishes and other animals still has its crypto-Christian character. If we take the man in a boat being attacked by a sea monster to be Jonah, we even witness here an overt early Christian symbol of eternal life.

In the conch of the main apse is a large 11th-century fresco, the Madonna enthroned with the Christ child and symbols of the Evangelists. To the right, Sts. Hermagoras (selected, according to tradition, by St. Mark himself as the first bishop of Aquileia), Fortunatus, and Euphemia, the little prince Henry, the German Emperor Conrad II (crowned in Rome, 1027), and the Empress Gisela. Left, Sts. Mark, Hilary, and Tazanius, and with them Bishop Poppo offering the Virgin a model of the church. The left apsidiole shows three rows of 11th-century frescoes, which are much damaged.

The crypt of the basilica has fine Byzantine and Benedictine frescoes, probably of the closing 12th century.

Grado. Connected with the mainland by a causeway, Grado was a sort of summer resort of Aquileia during the period of its growth, and served as a place of refuge for its inhabitants when Attila attacked their city in 452 and again when the Lombards came in 568. It was at this latter time that the Aquileians fortified Grado. Aquileia's own Bishop Paolino I took up residence there, keeping the title of Patriarch, which he had conferred upon himself. In 607 the Lombardic Arians of Aquileia appointed their own patriarch, and by the middle of the 8th century Rome recognized both patriarchs. Though the Patriarch of Grado lived in Venice after 1105, the Patriarchate of Grado was only abolished in 1451, and definitely turned into the Patriarchate of Venice as it remains today. Grado's role, however, was played out after the 12th century.

The town has two interesting basilicas dating back to its period of glory.

The Basilica of S. Eufemia, whose relics, like those of St. Hermagoras, had been brought to Grado, was consecrated in 579 by Bishop Elias. It was built of materials taken from an older building, including fragments of a 4th/5th-century basilica.

The mosaic floor is of the time of the present building; under it are remains of the older basilica, which can be seen by opening a trap door.

To the left of the building is a baptistery of the second half of the 5th century.

The Basilica di S. Maria delle Grazie, built in the 4th/5th centuries, was done over in the 6th century and, after a baroque rebuilding, was restored in 1929. It has Byzantine capitals. From the floor of the right nave one can look down on some remnants of floor mosaics of the original church.

Cividale. While the Lombardic art of Cividale is highly interesting, and its museum contains some Byzantine objects worth seeing, particular mention should be made here of a remarkable sculpture of Byzantine Eastern style, to be seen in the so-called Lombard Tempietto, the small church of S. Maria delle Valle, which sits in a romantic spot right beside the river Natisone, with the Julian Alps in the background. This consists of stucco figures of six female saints, presented in a Syrian style, dressed as Byzantine patricians, and surrounded by ornamental decoration also in stucco.

Figures and decor must have been brought hither and might well have been executed by a Byzantine artist. Byzantine sculpture of this kind is extremely rare, and these examples should not be missed. They are now generally dated 8th century or earlier; the fact that they are made of stucco may also indicate that they were copies.

Under the six statues is an arch, also of stucco in Eastern style, containing a much damaged fresco of Christ with the archangels Michael and Gabriel. To the sides of the arch are frescoes of martyrs (since the time of our visit, these, like other frescoes in the apse, may have been detached for restoration). In the old sacristy are classic and medieval stone fragments.

Poreč (Parenzo). The Basilica of Euphrasius, in Poreč, is a most interesting monument, which can easily be visited from Trieste. Koper (Capodistria) near Trieste is a center of busses and there are hotel accommodations in Poreč. With a car, one can make it from Trieste and back in a day.

The Basilica of Euphrasius is of interest, in the first place, for its history. In the beginning of the 3rd century there was a "house church" here in a secular building; in its floor we still see a splendid mosaic of a fish, the early Christian symbol (illustrated on p. 30). By the end of the 4th century a new church had been built; this building, too, had floor mosaics, which can be seen by opening trap doors in the floor of the present church. Thereafter, in the first half of the 5th century, the first basilica was built, a part of the older church serving as narthex. At last, in the middle of the 6th century, Bishop Euphrasius built the present structure, at the time when Justinian recaptured Italy and the Justinian mosaics of Ravenna were set up. The new basilica included a feature not present in the first: in addition to the main apse, two apsidioles cut into the wall, opening a further opportunity for mosaics. Euphrasius was an ambitious man and fitted his cathedral out with mosaics, marble, and stucco, even using mother-of-pearl in the mosaics, a material most uncommon for this purpose. Nor did he miss the opportunity to appear in person in the apse mosaic and have his initials en-

S. Maria della Valle, Cividale: stucco female saints

Basilica of Euphrasius, Poreć: mosaic inside arch, with medallions of lamb and female saints

graved on certain capitals. Various columns have Byzantine capitals, and many of the carved stone decorations in the church are pure Byzantine.

The main mosaics are on the triumphal arch and in the apse. Above the arch, Christ sits on the globe, Apostles right and left. Inside the arch of the apse: above, the Lamb, and left and right, in descending order, female saints. In the apse, the Madonna enthroned, with Christ child, guarded by two archangels; further right, three saints; further left, St. Maur presenting Euphrasius to the Virgin; the bishop, accompanied by the archdeacon Claudius and the latter's little son Euphrasius, offers her the church. The lower cycle shows the Annunciation (the Virgin spinning purple wool; see p. 35) and the Visitation, with the indiscreet servant eavesdropping on the conversation of the holy women (p. 35).

In the left apsidiole, there is a mosaic of Christ. The ciborium, built in 1277, shows an Annunciation of that period.

All the mosaics are in excellent condition. They belong to the rare examples from the period of Justinian, and their subjects as well as their style provide an excellent introduction to Byzantine art of later periods.

Basilica of Euphrasius, Poreć: left, detail of apse mosaic, showing Madonna enthroned; right, detail of Visitation mosaic, showing the eavesdropping servant

IN CONCLUSION

ART TODAY is gradually losing, has in fact to a great extent already lost, its national and regional character. Modern painting and architecture have come to look more and more the same the world over. Art historians of the future may hardly find it profitable to study the influence of the fading national or regional stylistic features; they will confine their research in depth to products of a more distant past. Time will show whether what we have gained in this process of equalization and the diminishing of national characteristics will outweigh what we have sacrificed in local values to the ever-growing speed and facility of communication.

In Byzantium's time the contacts between nations still allowed adaptation and acceptance of alien styles, and this produced happy results in a slow blending of cultural values. Byzantine values continued to interest the non-Byzantine world. This process of penetration and absorption of Byzantine values was gradual, for the

182

most part, but sometimes it was either accelerated or interrupted by sudden great events—such as, for example, Russia's adoption of the Orthodox faith, which introduced to Russia the Byzantine art so closely linked with that religion. The Crusades, damaging though they were to Byzantium, nevertheless suddenly stimulated new contacts between West and East. The Arab explosion, on the other hand, abruptly cut off relations between Byzantium and part of the Eastern world.

As to Italy, the ties between the Western and Eastern halves of the old Roman Empire proved strong enough to permit an enduring contact between the two, whatever the events or circumstances. In consequence, Italy, meeting-place of West and East, provides an ideal ground for study of this encounter. Rome, hub of the world in the classic era, recovered its international importance in Christian times and enabled Italy, notwithstanding its divisions and the conquests of foreign invaders, to preserve its stature as a clearing-house for Western and Eastern culture. Though Western Europe of course had its direct contacts with the Byzantine Empire at various times and in various ways, Italy kept an indirect relationship alive between the two by transmitting to the Western world its regional art strongly influenced by Byzantium and full of Byzantine motives.

Even after Byzantium disappeared as a state, it continued as a living influence. As Professor Ostrogorsky expresses it so movingly in his *History of the Byzantine State:*

> Byzantium fell in 1453 but her spirit remained. Her faith, her culture, and her conception of political life lived on and their influence was felt not only in those lands which had once been Byzantine, but beyond the old frontiers of the Empire, acting as a stimulus to the civilization of European nations.

It was natural that after its disappearance as a state Byzantium should remain a living factor in European culture. While the Slavic Orthodox countries continued their Byzantine traditions, Italy, though Western and not Orthodox, had been so long exposed to Byzantium that, in its cultural relations with other parts of the West, it could hardly fail to keep impressing upon them the marks of its historic contacts with the Eastern Empire. Thus Italy continued to play its part in spreading Byzantine culture, as it had done in the days of Byzantium's existence.

BIBLIOGRAPHY

THE NUMBER OF BOOKS on the history, religion, and art of Byzantium is very great, and still growing, offering those interested in the empire an unlimited opportunity to increase their knowledge. We have tried to prepare a limited list of books of interest to the reader of this volume, hoping that such a list will lead him to many more books.

GENERAL HISTORY OF BYZANTIUM

GEORGE OSTROGORSKY, *History of the Byzantine State,* 548 pp., Oxford: Basil Blackwell, 1956.

> A newer edition has appeared in German (*Geschichte des byzantinischen Staates,* 514 pp., Munich: C. H. Beck, 1963). Professor Ostrogorsky's book is an excellent work, and is also so organized as to enable the reader to look up special points of interest.

A. A. VASILIEV, *History of the Byzantine Empire, 324–1453*, 846 pp., Madison: University of Wisconsin Press, 1952 (also paperback).
> Also a standard work, organized in great part according to special subjects.

STEVEN RUNCIMAN, *Byzantine Civilization*, 320 pp., London: Edward Arnold, 1948 (also Meridian paperback).
> Dealing with special aspects of Byzantium, though also giving a short general historical outline.

PAUL LEMERLE, *Histoire de Byzance*, 127 pp., Paris: Presses Universitaires de France, 1956.
> The above, and the two titles next below, give a short but very clear picture of Byzantine history.

J. M. HUSSEY, *The Byzantine World*, 191 pp., London: Hutchinson University Library, 1957.

NORMAN H. BAYNES, *The Byzantine Empire*, 256 pp., Oxford: University Press, 1958.

NORMAN H. BAYNES and H. ST. L. B. MOSS, *Byzantium: An Introduction to East Roman Civilization*, 436 pp., Oxford: Clarendon Press, 1948.
> A series of articles on specific subjects by various authors, with several black-and-white photos.

ERNEST STEIN, *Histoire du Bas-Empire*, 3 vols., 1572 pp., Paris: Desclée de Brouwer, 1949–59.
> Gives a beautiful description of the pre-Byzantine Roman Empire from 284 to 565, explaining the factors that contributed to the formation of Byzantium.

LYNN WHITE, JR., ed., *The Transformation of the Roman World: Gibbon's Problem after Two Centuries*, 321 pp., Berkeley: University of California Press, 1966.
> Although paying due respect to Gibbon, the lucid essays in this book explain the weaknesses of his approach that, along with his lack of information subsequently available, prevented him from seeing Byzantium as "a new phenomenon with its own characteristics."

SPECIAL SUBJECTS
IN THE HISTORY OF BYZANTIUM

The Life of Constantine the Great

As views on Constantine differ so much, it is useful to study books by different authors, such as the several listed below.

JACOB BURCKHARDT, *Die Zeit Constantins des Grossen,* 432 pp. Basel: G. B. Fischer, 1954 (also Anchor paperback, tr. Moses Hadas).

JOSEPH VOGT, *Constantin der Grosse und sein Jahrhundert (Biblio-thek der Weltgeschichte),* 303 pp., Munich: Münchner Verlag, 1949.

ANDRÉ PIGANIOL, *L'Empereur Constantin,* 247 pp., Paris: Rieder, 1932.

Galla Placidia

VITO ANTONIO SIRAGO, *Galla Placidia e la trasformazione politica dell' occidente,* 566 pp., Louvain: Publications Universitaires, 1961.

The Life of Justinian the Great

CHARLES DIEHL, *Justinien et la civilisation byzantine au VIe siècle,* 2 vols., 679 pp., New York: Burt Franklin, 1959 (reprint of 1901 edition).

GLANVILLE DOWNEY, *Constantinople in the Age of Justinian,* 181 pp., Norman: University of Oklahoma Press, 1960.

Ravenna

CHARLES DIEHL, *Études sur l'administration byzantine dans l'exarchat de Ravenne (560–751),* 695 pp., New York: Burt Franklin, 1959 (reprint of 1888 edition).

Includes a bibliography.

The Barbarians

GABRIELE PEPE, *Il medio evo barbarico d'Italia,* 353 pp., Turin: G. Einaudi, 1963.

As the medieval history of Italy is so closely connected with the history of the barbarian conquerors, especially with that of the Lombards, this book will be very useful.

Southern Italy

JULES GAY, *L'Italie méridionale et l'empire byzantin depuis l'avène-ment de Basile I jusqu'à la prise de Bari par les Normands (867–1071),* 2 vols., 636 pp., New York: Burt Franklin, 1960 (reprint of 1904 edition).

After giving a general view of the Byzantine South of Italy before Basil I came to the throne of Byzantium, this book continues the very complicated story of this region of Italy in its ever-changing relations with Byzantium, the Lombards, the Pope, the Franks, the Arabs, and finally the Normans.

The Arabs

A. A. VASILIEV, *Byzance et les arabes,* 3 vols., resp. 451, 440, 296 pp., Brussels: Institut de Philologie et d'Histoire Orientale, 1935 & 1950.

PHILIP K. HITTI, *The Arabs,* 274 pp., Chicago: Gateway, 1949; new edition (paperback), 1956.

The Crusades

STEVEN RUNCIMAN, *A History of the Crusades,* 3 vols., resp. 377, 523, 530 pp., Cambridge: University Press, 1951–55.

> A classic in this field.

RELIGION

> The history of Byzantium is so interwoven with the history of the Orthodox Church that each general book on Byzantine history goes deeply into church matters. Yet there is, of course, an enormous literature—both general and specific— in the field of religion; a small selection follows here.

R. M. FRENCH, *The Eastern Orthodox Church,* 186 pp., London: Hutchinson University Library, 1957.

> A small book, but a useful introduction.

W. H. C. FREND, *The Donatist Church,* 360 pp., Oxford: Clarendon Press, 1952.

> Explains the Donatist movement, which, at the beginning of the life of the Church, touched principles of great importance to its organization.

FRANCIS DVORNIK, *The Ecumenical Councils,* 112 pp., New York: Hawthorn Books, 1961.

> An authoritative book on the councils that played such a great role in the history of the empire.

WALTER NORDEN, *Das Papsttum und Byzanz,* 764 pp., New York: Burt Franklin, 1958 (reprint of 1903 edition).

> Deals with the relationship between Byzantium and the popes.

STEVEN RUNCIMAN, *The Eastern Schism,* 189 pp., Oxford: Clarendon Press, 1956.

> Deals with the schism of 1054 between the Eastern and Western churches, and the situation in the 11th and 12th centuries—a book useful for understanding the growing differences between the churches.

JOSEPH GILL, S. J., *The Council of Florence,* 457 pp., Cambridge:

University Press, 1961.

>An interesting account of the final act in the relationship between the two churches.

ADRIAN FORTESCUE, *The Uniate Eastern Churches*, 244 pp., New York: Frederick Ungar, 1923.

>As the visitor to Italy encounters Uniate churches on the mainland and in Sicily, this book may be of interest.

Reference Books on Religion

>In addition to his Bible, the student of Byzantine art will want to have at his disposal the following books.

The Apocryphal New Testament, transl. by Montague Rhodes James, 594 pp., Oxford: Clarendon Press, 1955.

The Fourteen Books of the Apocrypha (Old Testament), ed. by Manuel Komroff, 350 pp., New York: Tudor, 1949.

A concordance, such as Alexander Cruden, *Complete Concordance,* 783 pp., New York: Holt, Rinehart & Winston, 1949.

The Oxford Dictionary of the Christian Church, 1492 pp., London: Oxford University Press, 1957.

HELEN ROEDER, *Saints and their Attributes,* 391 pp., London: Longmans, Green, 1955.

HANS FREIHERR VON CAMPENHAUSEN, *Griechische Kirchenväter,* 172 pp., Stuttgart: W. Kohlhammer, 1956.

ART

General

CHARLES DIEHL, *Manuel d'art byzantin,* 2nd edition, 2 vols., 946 pp., Paris: Auguste Picard, 1925–26.

>Contains an enormous amount of information on Byzantine art. Though further studies may have made some of Diehl's judgments obsolete, and although some of the monuments he describes have disappeared through war damage, the book still has great value; unfortunately, it is difficult to obtain.

ANDRÉ GRABAR, *La Peinture byzantine,* 201 pp., Geneva: Skira, 1953 (also in English).

>Many color plates. Deals with Byzantine art in several countries; in Italy, it describes and shows monuments in Rome, Rossano, Cefalù, Palermo, Ravenna, Venice, and Torcello.

DAVID TALBOT RICE, *Byzantine Art,* rev. ed., 272 pp., Baltimore: Penguin Books, 1954.

This book, with many plates, deals with Byzantine art in general and with many examples of Byzantine art in Italy.

JOHN BECKWITH, *The Art of Constantinople,* 184 pp., New York: Phaidon, 1961.

> One of the most recent books on the subject, with many plates, and a chronological table that the reader will find very useful.

OTTO DEMUS, *Byzantine Mosaic Decoration,* 97 pp., London: Routledge, Kegan Paul, 1953.

> An excellent introduction to Byzantine mosaics, of which a number are to be found in Italy; many plates.

RODOLPHE GUILLAND, *Mosaïques byzantines en Italie,* 22 pp., Paris: Plon, 1952.

> Gives a good short account of Byzantine mosaics in Italy; with 14 large color plates.

CHARLES RUFUS MOREY, *Mediaeval Art,* 412 pp., New York: W. W. Norton, 1942.

> The first half of this book contains much information on Byzantine influence in Italy.

CHARLES RUFUS MOREY, *Christian Art,* 120 pp., New York: W. W. Norton, 1958 (paperback).

> A useful small book, with several illustrations; the first part relates to the subject of the present volume.

Early Christian Monuments

F. VAN DER MEER and CHRISTINE MOHRMANN, *The Atlas of the Early Christian World,* 216 pp., London: Thomas Nelson & Sons, 1958.

> A most useful guide to the early Christian monuments, this book includes a wealth of information in its text, as well as maps and countless plates dealing with Christianity from its beginnings up to the 7th century. Since much of that period concerns Rome, the visitor interested in that city's early Christian monuments cannot do without this book in preparing his pilgrimage.

O. M. DALTON, *Early Christian Art,* 386 pp., Oxford: Clarendon Press, 1925.

> With many plates, this book gives an elaborate survey of its subject, including, of course, Italy.

DAVID TALBOT RICE, *The Beginnings of Christian Art,* 223 pp., London: Hodder and Stoughton, 1957.

> Not only describes the earliest period, but carries on into the 14th century; with a number of plates.

CHARLES RUFUS MOREY, *Early Christian Art,* 296 pp., Princeton: University Press, 1953.

> Will be found most helpful in understanding the period from the beginnings up to the 8th century.

ANDRÉ GRABAR, *Le premier art chrétien (200–395)* (*L'Univers des formes*), 326 pp., Paris: Gallimard, 1966.

> In this volume, Professor Grabar discusses the budding Christian art, still based so much on Roman style, and provides a profusion of photographs, many in color, of the art of the catacombs and other monuments of the period.

W. F. VOLBACH and M. HIRMER, *Early Christian Art,* 364 pp., New York: Abrams, 1961.

> An instructive text, with a great many beautiful photographs, covering the story of early Christian art up to the 7th century. It deals with many subjects of the present volume.

The Influence of Byzantine Art on Western Art

ANDRÉ GRABAR AND CARL NORDENFALK, *Early Mediaeval Painting,* 242 pp., New York: Skira, 1957.

ANDRÉ GRABAR and CARL NORDENFALK, *Romanesque Painting,* 232 pp., New York: Skira, 1958.

> Both these beautifully illustrated books deal with periods contemporary with Byzantium and will be very helpful in following Byzantine influence on the West.

MARIO ROTILI, *Origini della pittura italiana,* 108 pp., Bergamo: Istituto Italiano d'Arti Grafiche, 1963.

> Related, for the greater part, to the subject of our volume; with many plates, including excellent color.

Books Dealing with Specific Monuments (listed in the sequence followed in this volume)

OTTAVIO MORISANI, *Gli Affreschi di S. Angelo in Formis,* 91 pp., Naples: di Mauro, 1962.

> Gives a full description of the monument, with a great many plates, some in color.

ALBA MEDIA, *Gli Affreschi delle cripte eremitiche pugliesi,* 270 pp. and volume of plates, Rome: Collezione Meridionale Editrice, 1939.

> A most valuable guide to the frescoes in these often remote crypts.

OTTO DEMUS, *The Mosaics of Norman Sicily,* 478 pp., London: Routledge, Kegan Paul, 1949.

This is among the books one would like to take along to Sicily, but, alas, the airlines make such things rather difficult. Many plates.

ERNST KITZINGER, *The Mosaics of Monreale*, 132 pp., Palermo: S. F. Flaccovio, 1960.

As well as a great number of color plates, this book includes an index of the principal Monreale mosaic cycles, enabling the reader to go thoroughly into the splendor of the cathedral.

JOSEPH DEÈR, *The Dynastic Porphyry Tombs of the Norman Period in Sicily*, 188 pp., Cambridge, Mass.: Harvard University Press, 1959.

This book should provide anyone interested in this fascinating subject with all he could want. With plates.

BIAGIO PACE, *I Mosaici di Piazza Armerina*, 119 pp., Rome: Gherardo Casini, 1955.

The text and the many plates give an interesting picture of this monument, the date of which is contemporary with many examples of Christian art.

KURT WEITZMANN, *The Fresco Cycle of S. Maria di Castelseprio*, 101 pp., Princeton: University Press, 1951.

Professor Weitzmann gives a thorough analysis of this intriguing monument. Many plates.

GUISEPPE BOVINI, *Principale bibliografia su Ravenna romana, paleocristiana e paleobizantina*, 46 pp., Ravenna: Istituto di Antichità Ravennati e Bizantine, 1965.

A bibliography of writings about the history and the artistic monuments of Ravenna.

OTTO DEMUS, *The Church of S. Marco in Venice*, 236 pp., Washington: Dumbarton Oaks Research Library and Collection, 1960.

This book deals with the historical background of Venice in relation to the church, its architecture, and its sculpture. Many plates. It may be expected that a book by Professor Demus on the mosaics of the church will follow in the not-too-remote future.

PIETRO TOESCA and FERNANDO FORLATI, *Mosaics of St. Mark's*, 51 pp., New York: New York Graphic Society, 1958.

The text and the many plates (both black-and-white and color) afford good preparation for seeing the church mosaics.

GIOVANNI LORENZONI, *La Pala d'oro di S. Marco* (*Forma e colore*, 7), 53 pp., Florence: Sadea-Sansoni, 1965.

Includes 47 color plates.

GUIDE BOOKS

Guida d'Italia, Milan: Touring Club Italiano.

    The various volumes of this series are excellent sources of information on the monuments, and should, if possible, be taken on the journey. The following volumes are relevant to the areas discussed in the present book:

Vol.   6 *Venezia e dintorni* (1951)
Vol.   8 *Friuli—Venezia Giulia* (1963)
Vol. 10 *Emilia e Romagna* (1957)
Vol. 16 *Roma e dintorni* (1962)
Vol. 18 *Campania* (1963)
Vol. 19 *Napoli e dintorni* (1960)
Vol. 20 *Puglia* (1962)
Vol. 21 *Basilicata e Calabria* (1965)
Vol. 22 *Sicilia* (1953)

J. M. WIESEL, *Rom: ein Kunst- und Reiseführer,* Stuttgart: W. Kohlhammer, 1960.

    This guide gives, among other things, a résumé of the various periods of art, in specialized chapters giving the monuments from each period.

INDEX OF PLACES